THE CURRICULUM
THEORY AND PRACTICE

A.V. KELLY

Harper & Row, Publishers

London   New York   Hagerstown   San Francisco

Copyright © 1977 A. V. Kelly

First published 1977
Harper & Row Ltd
28 Tavistock Street
London WC2E 7PN

British Library Cataloguing in Publication Data

Kelly, Albert Victor
    The curriculum.
    1. Education — Curriculum
    I. Title
    375   LB1570

ISBN 0-06-318053-7
ISBN 0-06-318054-5   Pbk

Designed by Richard Dewing, Millions
Typeset by Preface Ltd, Salisbury
Printed by A. Wheaton & Company, Exeter

Contents

Acknowledgements

No work is the product of one man and this book is no exception. My thanks are therefore due to many people who have contributed to the thinking I have here tried to put into words. My M.A. students have provided a regular forum for the clarification of my thoughts and have kept those thoughts firmly welded to the practice of education. Alan Beck, John Handford and Vincent Hughes provided comments on the first draft of the book which were both encouraging and constructively helpful in many ways; I hope they will recognize their hands in some of the adjustments I have made. My particular thanks must also go to my three colleagues in the Curriculum Studies field at Goldsmiths' College, Geva Blenkin, Meriel Downey and Carol Pudwell, who helped me throughout with advice, comment and — not of least value — continuous support and encouragement. All of these must be given a share of whatever credit the book earns but no responsibility for any criticism it attracts. Finally, a special word of thanks must go to Dorma Urwin without whose miraculous ability to transform my scribbled manuscript — often beyond my own powers to decipher — into beautiful typescript it is doubtful if the work would ever have been completed.

A. V. Kelly

'Children should always show great
forbearance toward grown-up people.'

Antoine de Saint-Expéry, *The Little Prince*

Foreword

In recent years the curriculum industry on both sides of the Atlantic has expanded enormously as we have witnessed the arrival of planned curriculum development and all of the schemes both theoretical and practical which that has spawned. Never before has the substance of education been analysed, dissected and examined in every part of its anatomy in such detail and never before has there been such rapid and widespread change in educational practice. It must also be admitted that these two developments have not always been in phase. The gap between theory and practice remains a large and ugly chasm.

As a result of this rapid growth, there has been a proliferation of books on the curriculum. To add to their number, therefore, requires justification and that can only be found if something genuinely different is being attempted. This book tries to be different in two broad but related ways.

In the first place, most of the books that are written on the curriculum deal with one specific aspect of Curriculum Theory — the common curriculum, curriculum integration, curriculum evaluation and so on. Many of them are also written in support of particular theories or to argue specific cases. This book attempts to offer an overview by considering together many of the theories that are offered in this area and attempting to provide the reader with the understanding he needs to weigh them against each other.

If the book does argue a specific case — and it could hardly avoid doing so — that case is the centrality of the teacher's role in curriculum development and the need to support him in this role. It is written in the belief and it attempts to establish the thesis that control of curriculum development will always effectively rest in the hands of the teacher in the classroom and that the sooner we recognize this and begin to find appropriate ways of supporting him the sooner curriculum development will take off.

A second purpose of this book is to contribute to this support for the teacher. For it attempts to make available to him in a form that he can assimilate some of the theories that abound in this area in such a way as to help him to develop the kind of theoretical understanding that he will need if his practical provision is to have real effect and if the gap between theory and practice, which is death to any educational development, is ever to be bridged.

In short, this book sets out to do for Curriculum Theory what *Theory and Practice of Education: An Introduction* tried to do for Education Theory in general and to use the approach adopted there to explore those problems of curriculum design which lie at the heart of all educational debate. For unless appropriate links can be forged between the theory and the practice of education and the teacher's confidence in the perspectives that theoretical considerations can offer him can be reaffirmed, there can be no effective curriculum development no matter how hard people try from outside the school to promote it.

This book is offered as a small contribution to that great cause.

A. V. Kelly
London, February 1977

CHAPTER 1

CURRICULUM PLANNING

It is stating the obvious to assert that education has changed drastically in the last twenty or thirty years. Both in the United Kingdom and elsewhere the provision of educational opportunities has been extended and many resultant modifications have become necessary to all aspects of the education system. Nor is it surprising that the nature and structure of our education system should have been changing so extensively at a time when we have been experiencing social change of an equally dramatic kind, much of it prompted by rapid technological advance. The education system is a social institution which should be expected to change along with other such institutions. It would be more surprising, not to say disturbing, if the education system were to stand still while all else changed and it is this that renders incomprehensible the efforts of those conservatives who wish to see educational change arrested or even advocate a return to former systems, the suitability of which even to the times that spawned them is often difficult to discern.

Amidst all of this change, nothing has been more significant nor as fundamental as the major modifications that have been made to the curriculum. The significance of this lies in the fact that it has manifested itself at all levels of educational activity, from the nursery school through to the university, from the education of the least able pupils to that of the most educationally gifted. Its fundamental nature derives from the fact that the curriculum is the very foundation of any education system and no amount of tinkering with the structure of the system, the organization of schools or the selection procedures to be used will have more than a peripheral effect unless accompanied by a re-thinking of the real substance of education — the curriculum itself.

And so, while changes to the structure of the system (such as the introduction of comprehensive schools and of mixed ability classes) have attracted the main attention of the man in the street, it has rightly been the curriculum itself that has been the focus of attention for the professional teacher, since without an understanding of what has been happening in that sphere the other changes make little sense and, indeed, have little point. Most of these changes, for example, have been directed towards the attainment of educational equality and a fairer distribution of educational provision, but it is only through the curriculum itself and not through mere organizational changes that this will be achieved.

One feature that has characterized this curriculum change of recent years and which must be realized at the outset of this discussion is the increased incidence of planning and preparation in curriculum development. Most of the curriculum change that we have seen in the past has been of a kind best described as unplanned 'drift' (Hoyle 1969a) and a good deal of this still goes on. Recently, however, educationists have begun to see the need for planned innovation, to recognize that if educational change is to keep pace with and match changes in society, it must be deliberately managed rather than merely left to happen. To recognize this is not, of course, to be committed to a totally revolutionary approach to curriculum development. The advantages of evolution over revolution are at least as evident in education as elsewhere. It is, however, to acknowledge that the process of evolution can be smoother, quicker and more effective, if it is not left to chance but implemented according to carefully thought-out strategies. It is this that makes the kind of understanding of curriculum development that can come from a deep study of Curriculum Theory the most essential item in the armoury of the modern teacher.

It is the aim of this chapter to identify what is involved in this, to outline some of the essential ingredients both of the study of Curriculum Theory and the practice of curriculum planning. Almost all of these points will be examined in greater detail in the chapters that follow, but an overall framework, a rationale, a cognitive map offered at the outset may help to establish and maintain the interrelationship of the many factors involved in curriculum development. For not the smallest problem facing the teacher as he recognizes his responsibility for curriculum planning is the range of interconnected factors that he must constantly keep in balance. Like a juggler he must not only keep many balls in the air at the same time, he must also maintain the proper relationships between them if disaster is not to ensue.

What is the curriculum?

The first need is to achieve some clarity over what we are to understand by the term 'curriculum'. It is a term which is used with several meanings and a number of different definitions of it have been offered, so that it is important that we establish at the beginning what it should be taken to signify throughout this book.

To begin with, it will be helpful if we distinguish the use of the word to denote the content of a particular subject or area of study from the use of it to refer to the total programme of an educational institution. Often, of course, conflicts do arise as we try to reconcile the competing demands of these two aspects of curriculum planning and it may be that some of the inadequacies of previous attempts at curriculum planning can be attributed to the fact that it has tended to proceed in a rather piecemeal way within subjects rather than according to some overall rationale, so that the curriculum can be seen as 'the amorphous product of generations of tinkering' (Taba 1962, p. 8). Both of these dimensions of curriculum development are, of course, important, but it is the rationale of the total curriculum that must have priority since it would seem that once that is established on a firm basis, the curriculum of individual subjects should fall into place. At the very least, then, the total curriculum must be accorded prior consideration and it may be claimed that the main task that currently faces curriculum planners is to work out a basis on which some total scheme can be built.

Since it seems that this should be the main concern, this will be the focus of our discussion in this book and we will understand by the term 'curriculum' this overall rationale for the educational programme of the institution, and these general features of curriculum change and development, although much of what is said about curriculum development in this sense will, of course, be of relevance to the problems of developments within individual subject areas.

A further question that needs to be resolved is whether we are to place any limit on the kinds of school activity that we will allow to count as part of the curriculum. Again, the word can be found in use in a number of different contexts and again we need to distinguish these clearly.

For example, some educationists speak of the 'hidden curriculum', by which they mean those things which pupils learn at school because of the way in which the work of the school is planned and organized but which are not in themselves overtly included in the planning or even in the consciousness of those responsible for the school arrangements. Social roles, for example, are learnt, it is claimed, in this way, as are sex roles and attitudes to many other aspects of living. Implicit in any set of arrangements are the attitudes and values of those who create them, and these will be communicated to pupils in this accidental and perhaps even sinister way.

Some would argue that the values implicit in the arrangements made by schools for their pupils are quite clearly in the consciousness of some teachers and planners and are equally clearly accepted by them as part of what pupils should learn in school, even though they are not overtly recognized by the pupils themselves. In other words, teachers deliberately plan the school's 'expressive culture'. In such instances, therefore, the curriculum is 'hidden' only to or from the pupils. If or where this is so, the values to be learnt clearly from a part of what the teachers plan for their pupils and must, therefore, be accepted as fully a part of the curriculum.

Others, however, take a less definite and perhaps less cynical line on this but wish nevertheless to insist that teachers do have a responsibility here. They accept that the values and attitudes learnt *via* the hidden curriculum are not directly intended by teachers, but believe that, since these things are being learnt as a by-product of what is planned, teachers should be aware of and accept responsibility for what is going on, for what their pupils are learning in this unplanned way (Barnes 1976).

There is no doubting the importance of this notion of the hidden curriculum nor the need for curriculum planners and teachers to keep its implications constantly before them. To use the term 'curriculum', however, to denote such kinds of learning is to render the planning of a total curriculum impossible since the term is being used here to include experiences that by definition have not been deliberately planned, and which cannot be so, at least without ceasing to be 'hidden' in the sense used. It would seem better therefore to confine the use of the word curriculum to those activities that are planned or are the result of some intentionality on the part of teachers and planners, and to deal with these other kinds of learning as the hidden results or by-products of the curriculum rather than as part of the curriculum itself.

Much the same point emerges when we consider the distinction that has sometimes been made between the official curriculum and the actual curriculum. By the official curriculum is meant what is laid down in syllabuses, prospectuses and so on, the actual curriculum being what is covered in the practice of the school. The difference between them may be conscious or unconscious, the cause of any mismatch being either a deliberate attempt by the teachers or others to deceive, to make what they offer appear more attractive than it really is, or merely the fact that, since 'teachers and pupils are human, the realities of any course will never fully match up to the hopes and intentions of those who have planned it.

Both of these distinctions are important and we would be foolish to go very far in our examination of the curriculum without acknowledging both the gaps that must inevitably exist between theory and practice and the predilection of some teachers for elaborate 'packaging' of their wares. If, however, we are to achieve a definition of the curriculum that will offer a firm basis for curriculum planning, we should probably confine ourselves at least initially to what teachers and others plan with the serious intention of carrying out. At the same time, we must not lose sight of the fact that curriculum study must ultimately be concerned with the relationship between these two views of the curriculum, between intention and reality, if it is to succeed in linking the theory and the practice of the curriculum (Stenhouse 1975).

Lastly, we must also recognize the distinction that is often drawn between the 'formal' curriculum and the 'informal' curriculum, between the formal activities for which the timetable of the school allocates specific periods of teaching time or which, as in the case of the primary school, are included in the programme of work to be covered in normal school hours, and those many informal activities that go on, usually on a voluntary basis, at lunchtimes, after school hours, at weekends or during holidays. These latter activities, — sports, clubs, societies, school journeys and the like — are often called 'extra-curricular' activities and this suggests that they should be seen as separate from, as over and above the curriculum itself.

The reasons for this, however, are difficult to discern unless they are those that derive from the time of the day or week when they take place or the nature of the voluntary participation that usually characterizes them. For activities of this kind are usually seen to have as much educational validity and point as any of the formal arrangements of the school. Indeed, some would even argue that in certain cases they have more point than many such arrangements. It was for this reason that the Newsom Report recommended that they 'ought to be recognized as an integral part of the total educational programme (§ 135) and that to this end they be included in the formal timetable of an extended day. It is also for this reason that educationists such as Charity James have suggested that they be regarded and planned as one element of the curriculum (James 1968). The inclusion of this kind of activity in the formal provision made by the school is also a major feature of the philosophy of many of those concerned with the present development of community schools (Cooksey 1972, 1976a, 1976b).

Again, it would seem that, if we are concerned with curriculum planning, it would be foolish to omit by our definition of the curriculum a whole range of activities which teachers plan and execute with deliberate aims and intentions. In looking at curriculum planning, therefore, there would appear to be nothing to be gained from leaving out of consideration any planned activity.

There is a more subtle way, however, in which definitions of the curriculum can exclude some of the activities that teachers and others plan for their pupils. Some of the definitions that are offered contain a very clear and loaded 'value' element; they are prescriptive rather than descriptive and they thus encourage the omission from our consideration in curriculum planning of a good many activities we ought in no way to be ashamed of including in our curriculum nor encouraged to forget or place lower down the scale of priorities. Thus a definition of the curriculum such as that offered by Paul Hirst who tells us, 'The term curriculum would seem, from its derivation, to apply most appropriately to the programme of activities, to the course to be run by pupils in being educated' (Hirst 1969, p. 143) excludes from our consideration all activities that do not contribute to the education of pupils. Since Hirst himself offers us a very clear view of what shall count as educational, this definition, taken as it stands, would prevent us in planning a curriculum from including a whole range of activities and experiences that we might well wish to include in our programme on grounds other than their educational value. Vocational preparation of various kinds, for example, might be excluded by such a definition.

The term 'educational' contains a 'value' element that renders such a definition prescriptive rather than merely descriptive and therefore preempts certain kinds of discussion within the overall planning of the curriculum.

The same sort of difficulty results from the acceptance of a definition such as that offered, albeit with qualifications and a promise of subsequent modification, by one of the Open University courses on the curriculum, which tells us 'A curriculum is the offering of socially valued knowledge, skills and attitudes made available to students through a variety of arrangements during the time they are at school, college or university' (Open University, Course E283, Unit 1, §2.2). The limitation of the scope of the curriculum planner to knowledge that is socially valued clearly introduces a prescriptive 'value' element that will preclude, in some societies more than in others, the consideration of certain kinds of activity and experience.

It may be argued that such a definition can be interpreted descriptively, as saying no more than that the content of any curriculum will in fact always consist of socially valued knowledge, skills and attitudes. Such a description may well be perfectly valid, although it is then little more than a truism. However, to define 'curriculum' in this way is to say that it must only consist of such content, so that its effect is to prescribe the inclusion or exclusion of certain kinds of content on grounds of their social value. Thus, since this is far from being an objective criterion of selection, it introduces from the outset the question of who is to decide what is socially valued, a question which should be left for later decision.

An implicit prescription in our definition can cause as much difficulty, then, if not more, than the explicit exclusion of certain categories of school activity.

What is needed is a definition that is both value-neutral and all-embracing to provide us with a framework which makes possible the joint planning of all the school activities. Hence we will find it better to seek for a definition such as that offered by John Kerr, who defines the curriculum as 'all the learning which is planned and guided by the school, whether it is carried on in groups or individually, inside or outside the school' (Kerr 1968, p. 16). Such a definition provides us with a reasonably secure basis for planning all the organized activities of a school.

This, however, is only a beginning since we have done no more than specify what our curriculum planning is to be concerned with. Before we can get down to it in any detail, a further analysis of what we mean by the curriculum is necessary, an analysis based on the nature of curriculum planning itself.

Rational curriculum planning

All rational activities are characterized by having both purposes and procedures, aims or goals and devices for achieving those aims or goals. Curriculum planning as a rational activity is no exception to this. Hence no attempt at curriculum planning is likely to be profitable unless it includes consideration both of the aims of the activity and the means by which it is hoped those aims will be realized. In fact, it has been suggested (Tyler 1949; Hirst 1969) that the curriculum has to be seen as consisting of at least three elements and curriculum planning, therefore, as having at least three dimensions — objectives, content or subject matter and methods or procedures. In short, we must distinguish in our curriculum planning what we are hoping to achieve, the ground we are planning to cover in order to achieve it and the kinds of activity that we consider likely to be most effective in helping us towards our goals. Some, such as Tyler himself, would add a further element — evaluation, an assessment of how successful we have been in attaining our ends. This is obviously an important and sensible addition and clearly has implications for the other three. In fact, as we shall argue in Chapter 5, it is an essential element in curriculum development. However, it would seem to be a contingent rather than a logically necessary element of rational curriculum planning, since, although it might be unwise, it would surely not be irrational to make no evaluation of the extent to which we have succeeded in our intentions. Certainly many major curriculum innovations have not accepted formal evaluation as an essential requirement.

This, then, it is claimed, is the logic of the curriculum and the only proper basis for rational curriculum planning. The force of the argument is increased also when in the light of this analysis one examines earlier forms of curriculum development. For it does seem true, as Hirst suggests, that the concern of the 'traditional' curriculum with content only, with subjects and subject matter, and the obsession of the 'progressive' curriculum with methods, with such things as projects and discovery learning, both reveal the inadequacies of any attempt at curriculum planning that does not pay due regard to all three of the elements outlined, and especially to the need for objectives of some kind, a need which appears to have been ignored by everyone.

This analysis, then, if taken just as it stands, would give us a very simple model for curriculum planning, a linear model which requires us to specify our objectives, to plan the content and the methods which will lead us towards them and, finally, perhaps to endeavour to measure the extent of our success. It is, however, too simple a model for many reasons, most of which will become apparent when we consider the problems of prespecified objectives in Chapter 2.

One reason why it will not suffice, which must be mentioned here, is that it does not make sufficient allowance for the interrelatedness of the separate elements. At the very least we must allow for the fact that the results of our evaluation processes may be used to modify our planning. Thus it has been suggested that we should employ a cyclical rather than a linear model'and link up evaluation with the framing of objectives to create a continuous cycle (Wheeler 1967).

This would seem to be a step in the right direction but many would claim that the influence of evaluation on curriculum planning should be a continuous process rather than being delayed until the exercise is over and, if we accept that, then we must expect such continuous evaluation to result in regular modifications of our planning. In fact, we must go further than this and acknowledge the interrelationship of all four elements, since the practical experience of most teachers suggests that every one of these four elements is constantly being modified by every other and that the whole business of curriculum planning must be seen as one of constant interaction between the elements. A more suitable model might therefore be derived from the idea of a permutated entry on a football pool with every possible kind of combination allowed for, or the physicist's notion of 'dynamic equilibrium' where stable progress is made possible by the balanced interaction of a variety of forces.

So much for the logic of curriculum planning, but, as Hirst rightly reminds us (Hirst 1969), logic of itself cannot take us very far and what we still lack is any kind of basis or set of criteria upon which we can make a selection of either our objectives or our content or our methods. It is to meet this difficulty that the more sophisticated models of the curriculum that we are offered have been designed. Some of them are highly complex, so much so that it is difficult to imagine their being of any real use to a practising teacher or a planner of real curricula. It does seem possible, however, to produce a model which retains some of the simplicity of the model that logical considerations have led us to but which also draws our attention to the importance of factors deriving from other sources. This is the aim of the model that Denis Lawton offers us which brings in certain philosophical, psychological and sociological considerations, as well as reminding us that we would be foolish to ignore the practical aspects and implications of any programme (Lawton 1973).

Lawton suggests that in planning a curriculum rationally we should frame our objectives and decide on appropriate content and procedures by reference to three main kinds of consideration. Firstly, we must take note of those considerations that derive from the nature of knowledge itself. It has been suggested that certain questions about the curriculum can be answered for us by an analysis of what knowledge is, the different forms of knowledge and the different kinds of logic that are said to exist (Hirst 1965). This is a view to which we must later give closer consideration, but it is enough if we acknowledge here the claim that the curriculum planner must pay due regard to this kind of argument. Secondly, it is claimed, we must take full account of the nature of the child or of the individual children for whom the curriculum is being planned. Some programmes have been put together without any reference to anything other than what knowledge was thought to be. Indeed, it was this feature of 'traditional' education that led some thinkers to that emphasis, perhaps even overemphasis, on the child himself that has characterized the 'progressive' or 'child-centred' movement in education. No adequate curriculum plan can emerge unless due regard is paid to what we know about cognitive growth and child development generally. Thirdly, Lawton suggests that our curriculum must take full account of the social situation, the pressures and the needs of the society of which the school is a part. It is this kind of consideration that has led to recent demands for relevance in the curriculum and, although the concept of relevance needs careful elucidation and analysis, few would wish to deny that a curriculum planned without reference to society would have little hope of achieving success, no matter how success was to be gauged.

Such a model, then, takes us considerably further towards an understanding of what is involved in curriculum planning. It has the real merit of recognizing that choices and selection have to be made and of suggesting some of the factors that we will need to keep in mind when we come to make these choices. But that is as far as it takes us and, indeed, it is as far as any model can take us. It leaves the most fundamental question of all unanswered. For it offers us a series of factors some of which will be in conflict with each other. Among the many kinds of consideration it draws our attention to we must decide which are to have priority and we need some basis for balancing and evaluating the inevitably competing claims that we will discover, for example, between the demands of the individual child and those of society.

In engaging in rational curriculum planning, therefore, we need to be clear about the logic of the process and we need to take full account of all those other factors that appear to have some relevance to our enterprise, but we also need some basis upon which we can make the necessary choices and selection, a set of criteria, a framework of values within which to work. This, as we shall see in subsequent chapters, will be far from easy to attain.

The model that Lawton offers us, however, does have the merit of recognizing that curriculum planning cannot go on in an intellectual vacuum, cut off from contact with the society and the culture in which it is being practised, that the curriculum planner must be aware not only of the logical constraints of the activity in which he is engaged but also of the social pressures to which he and the curriculum development he is trying to foster are subject. These pressures take a number of forms and it is as well to be aware at the outset of the more influential of them, so that we are not misled into believing that curriculum planning is merely a matter of the application of rationality and logic.

Other pressures on curriculum planning

It is perhaps worth noting first of all that the factors we are about to consider will have their impact on curriculum development whether we like it or not. Indeed, it is these factors that were at work in the past and still are at work in situations where curriculum change is the result of the kind of unplanned 'drift' we have already referred to. If teachers and others do not plan their curriculum, these are the forces that will control the direction and form of curriculum change. On the other hand, if curricula are to be planned realistically and planned change effected smoothly, these factors must be taken into account in the planning process. Again, evolution is to be preferred to revolution, which is often not only painful but also ineffective.

Curriculum development, then, is subject to a great many social pressures. These pressures are often subtle and it is not always easy to justify what they may lead to, but their presence and their influence must be recognized and acknowledged.

Firstly, we may note the pressures on the curriculum that derive from economic sources. There is no way which we can or should ignore the economic function of the education system. As the Crowther Report reminded us, education has to be seen, at least in part, as a national investment from which society is entitled to expect some return. For the most part, that return will take the form of the output of a sufficient number of young people who have acquired the knowledge and skills that society needs to maintain and extend its development. From this source, therefore, will come pressures for the introduction of certain kinds of subject into the curriculum, such as reading, mathematics, sciences and technological subjects, and perhaps the inclusion of certain kinds of objective to govern the way in which we approach all or most of what we teach. A good example of this is the transmutation of handicraft into design and technology which recent years have witnessed, a development which has been in part prompted by and is one instance of the wave of interest in and enthusiasm for 'creativity' that followed the launching by the Russians of Sputnik I, the first space probe, in 1957. Technological change, especially on the scale we have witnessed in recent years, must have very serious consequences for the planning of the curriculum, for it results in major changes in the kinds of knowledge that society wants its children to be given. Indeed, the whole of the development of state-provided education can be seen as the result of exactly this kind of economic pressure.

It also results, however, in demands for changes of a more fundamental kind, changes in the manner in which we encourage children to learn as well as the content of that learning. For one of the clearest lessons of the technological change of recent years, again well brought out by the Crowther Report and its notion of 'general mechanical ability', is that if the citizen of the future is to be able to adapt to the changes he will continue to experience, his education must provide him with the flexibility of mind necessary for this. The emphasis will therefore need to be on the development of understanding rather than on the acquisition of knowledge in any lesser sense, and the consequences of that for curriculum planners are far-reaching.

A similar point emerges when we consider a second, and perhaps more important, consequence of technological change — the social changes that it brings in its train. For technological change leads to changes in the values and norms of a society and thus to another source of pressure on the curriculum. As man discovers that he can do more, that he can influence more and exercise more control over his physical and social environment in the widest sense of those terms, he also realizes that there are important questions to be asked about what he *ought* to do, how he *ought* to influence his environment. Technological change raises new moral problems over such issues as birth control, abortion, organ transplantation, pollution and the ecological balance of nature.

The rapid technological change of recent years has therefore been accompanied by equally dramatic changes in the very fabric of society and these social and moral changes also have their impact on the development of the curriculum, as will quickly be apparent from an examination of what has been happening within religious education in recent years and the advent and development of such areas as moral education and social education.

Again too the very fact of such continuous change creates demands for changes in the manner of learning, a fact which explains why we are increasingly concerned that pupils should learn to solve their own moral problems rather than to accept pre-packaged solutions which are unlikely to be adequate when they come as adults to cope with moral issues that have not yet arisen and cannot yet be foreseen. Teachers cannot predict the sorts of problem with which pupils may be faced, so that they must educate them in such a way that they learn to work out their own solutions as and when it becomes necessary. The relationship between social change and curriculum change needs a good deal more careful analysis than it has as yet received, but that there are important considerations here for the curriculum planner cannot be doubted.

Lastly, we must note a point which leads on naturally from the one we have just considered. We must take full cognisance of the ideological pressures to which the curriculum planner is subject. In short, we must not ignore the political function of education. In sociological parlance, ideologies are value systems competing for power within a society. The very fact that several such ideologies can be discerned in most contemporary societies, that they are pluralist societies, has in itself implications for the way in which we plan a curriculum since it suggests that we should develop in children the ability to cope with competing systems rather than initiate them into any one such set of beliefs or values.

However, what is important here is that we recognize that such ideologies are and have always been a major influence on curriculum development from the days of the 'aristocratic' ideology, which perhaps lingers on in certain places, to more recent attempts to champion the cause of the 'lower orders' in education. A good many curriculum changes of recent years have been prompted by a concern over problems of social class differences, the social mobility function of education, and this continues to be a major source of pressure on curriculum planners not least through the work of those sociologists who have recently come to recognize that one major source of social inequality is the curriculum itself (Young 1971).

These general influences make their impact on the curriculum not only through the effect they have on everyone's thinking but also more directly through several kinds of agency. Some of these are completely overt and attempt to exert a direct influence on the development of the curriculum. Organizations such as the Schools Council in the United Kingdom have been set up with the deliberate purpose of exploring certain aspects of the curriculum and of developing new schemes or projects that it is hoped will lead to improvements in the quality and relevance of what is offered to pupils at all levels and in all aspects of their work in schools. From time to time also Consultative Committees, Royal Commissions or other committees of inquiry are set up quite formally by a government to look into certain aspects of education and to advise on changes that might with profit be effected. Often, of course, the published reports of these committees are largely concerned with questions of organization and administration but seldom can they ignore curriculum issues completely, since any attempt to do so or any failure to achieve a full understanding of these issues will vitiate any recommendations they make concerning the organizational and administrative matters themselves, as the James Report on Teacher Education, for example, made apparent. Thus some of these reports have led to quite dramatic changes in certain areas of the curriculum in some schools. The changes, not all of them for the better, brought about in the provision made in secondary schools in the United Kingdom for the 'less able' pupil as a result of the recommendations of the Newsom Report and the similar impact of the Plowden Report on the work of the primary schools should provide sufficient evidence of the degree of influence that such reports can exercise.

In considering overt attempts to contribute to curriculum change and development we must also remember the role that it is intended should be played by the Inspectorate, now significantly coming to be known as the Advisory Service, at both central and local government levels. These bodies are explicitly employed to advise educational institutions on the development of their curricula and to disseminate experience and ideas between institutions. A good deal of this work is now done also by Teachers' Centres, some of which act not only as institutions for the in-service training of teachers in the new skills required of them by some curriculum changes but also as centres for the interchange of ideas between teachers from different schools.

In addition to these agencies that have been established with the express purposes of contributing to curriculum development, there are other agencies whose impact on curriculum change is less overt but none the less influential; indeed, they may well be more important because their influence is indirect. If we can ignore the influence of certain commercial agencies such as publishers, these would seem to fall into two main categories which we might call the political or financial and the academic.

In some countries political influence on the curriculum is quite direct and decisions about curriculum content, method and even balance of subjects and allocation of time are made centrally, leaving the individual school very little discretion. There are examples of the same kind of direct central control to be found in the history of the development of education in the United Kingdom also and proposals for the reintroduction of such control in some areas of the curriculum are currently being made. At present, however, the only legal requirement that any school in England and Wales must adhere to in planning its curriculum is the inclusion of religious instruction and a daily act of worship in its programme. It would be naive, however, to assume that each school is completely free to make its own arrangements in all other areas. Managing or governing bodies have to be satisfied that the school is fulfilling its role in the community as they envisage it and these bodies consist largely of people with particular political interests. Finance too is a crucial factor. The way in which the moneys allocated to a school are spent is a matter for the governing body to determine and the granting of additional money for specific projects is at the discretion of local government, so that, in the ultimate, whether a school can or cannot pursue any particular line of innovation is a decision that rests with those who hold the purse strings.

The second main source of indirect influence on curriculum planning is the academic influence exercised by universities, colleges of education and other institutions of higher education. There are several aspects to this.

In the first place, what is done in schools depends very much on what the teachers in the schools have been prepared for by their initial courses of training, so that the kind of course offered by the institutions of teacher education will have an important impact on curriculum development. The teachers themselves, of course, can exercise some control over the content of these courses through their involvement in the planning and constructing of them, although in the United Kingdom this is likely to become more difficult or at least to require new machinery now that the Area Training Organizations have been broken up.

Secondly, institutions of higher education will continue to exercise a degree of control over what is taught, at least in secondary schools, through the entry requirements they set for admission to their courses. It would be quite wrong of any school to ignore these in planning a programme for pupils who are likely to want to go on to courses in other institutions, whether of higher or further education.

Thirdly, this influence is felt most obviously through the control exercised by the universities over the content of examination syllabuses. Indeed, it is the public examination which is recognized by all teachers as the most obvious source of external control over the curriculum. More often than not they see its effect largely as an inhibiting one, preventing them from effecting changes that they might otherwise bring about to improve the quality of what they are offering pupils. That the public examination can also initiate change, however, and encourage teachers to develop their work in directions that they might of themselves not have envisaged, can be seen from work that has been done in a number of areas, and perhaps particularly through the changes already referred to that have been brought about in the very concept of craft teaching in secondary schools by the new syllabuses that the University of London has set up for design and technology at both 'O' and 'A' levels of the GCE (Hicks 1976).

Both of these aspects of the influence exercised by public examination syllabuses highlight the close interrelationship of examination and curriculum and the need for the planning of both to be done jointly. This in turn suggests that it is important that teachers be more closely involved in the planning and conduct of public examinations. Indeed, an acceptance of this point was part of the rationale for the introduction of the CSE examination in the United Kingdom as a result of the Beloe Report of 1960. The various modes of assessment made available to teachers by this examination and the real involvement of teachers in the examining processes have done much to show how teachers can be given increased control over this particular source of influence on curriculum development. The lead thus established has been followed by some GCE Boards in certain subject areas and, indeed, in some cases joint GCE and CSE syllabuses have been approved and established, thus paving the way for the possible introduction of a single public examination at 16+ in the near future, a significant feature of which may well be extensive teacher involvement (Schools Council 1971a).

Curriculum development and the teacher

This brief discussion of the influence of the public examination on curriculum development brings us to a consideration of what is emerging as the most crucial factor in curriculum development, the role of the individual teacher and the individual school. The last, but by no means the least important factors we must consider in our brief initial survey of curriculum planning and development are those that derive from the local considerations operating in any given school or classroom. These are the factors that will in the end determine what the outcome shall be, in terms of the actual curriculum of the individual school, of the influences and pressures that we have been listing. To be effective, any particular curriculum innovation must 'take' with the school and become fully institutionalized (Hoyle 1969b) and it is becoming very clear that the extent to which any project will 'take' will depend on a whole range of local factors within each individual school. Thus it is increasingly apparent that real and effective curriculum development must go on within individual schools rather than by the creation of projects or other innovations hatched out in some central place detached from the realities of any actual school situation. The theory and practice of curriculum development must go hand in hand from the outset of any piece of planning; they cannot effectively be married up at a point when each has developed too far to be readily adapted to the other.

Several factors within the school are likely to be important here, local industrial and employment conditions, the social origins and interests of the pupils and their parents, the expectations the community in general has of the school, and so on. Quite the most significant of these factors, however, as has become apparent from a number of different sources in recent years, is the attitudes of the teachers within the school, since these will be crucial in determining the realities of what goes on at the level of the individual classroom, which, after all, is what ultimately decides the actual curriculum of the school.

The positive role of the individual teacher in curriculum development is still not clear and this needs to be given more attention than it has hitherto had and to be more thoroughly explored. That the individual teacher has a 'make or break' role in relation to the attempts of any outside body to bring about curriculum change, however, is now indisputable, nor is this surprising since, as we have just said, it is the individual teacher who has the task of bridging any gap that might exist between curriculum theory and curriculum practice.

It is clear that many teachers can and do sabotage attempts to introduce changes into the curriculum. Teachers are often accused of conservatism, of too great an attachment to tradition, to 'tried and trusted methods'. Such an attitude is understandable when one realizes that their standing often depends on the maintenance of those areas of knowledge and experience in which they have a recognized expertise. This emphasizes the need to improve in-service opportunities so as to enable teachers to become rather less dependent on the skills and expertise they acquire in their initial courses. While such opportunities do not exist, however, the traditionalism of some teachers will remain a factor that we ignore at our peril in attempting to change any aspect of the curriculum of any school.

The converse of this is equally important. The degree to which any change that we attempt to introduce into a school is likely to be effective will largely be determined by the extent to which individual teachers become committed to it. There is simply no point in a Schools Council project team, a head teacher or even an enthusiastic group of teachers attempting to introduce some new scheme into a school's programme unless it has the support at least of all those teachers who will need to be involved in the implementation of it and preferably a good many other teachers as well, since saboteurs can work from without as well as from within. In particular, of course, it is vital that a project has the support of the head teacher and other senior staff, such as heads of relevant departments, heads of sections within the school, such as year groups and so on.

Nowhere has the truth of this been so manifest as in the attempts of some secondary schools in the United Kingdom in recent years to introduce mixed ability forms of grouping. This kind of innovation involves major changes of method and approach so that its success hinges on the willingness of individual teachers to adapt their methods and approaches to the requirements of the new situation. Unless teachers are willing to undertake this, and in the first instance to do so with a good deal of enthusiasm, or at least tolerance of the initial difficulties that must inevitably be experienced, it is better not to attempt to make the change at all. The importance of the individual teacher to the success or failure of this particular innovation in primary schools was one of the most significant findings of the major research project undertaken by the National Foundation for Educational Research in this field (Barker-Lunn 1970).

It will be clear, then, that if the role of the teacher is as central as this to successful curriculum development, no attempt to establish innovations derived from outside agencies will be successful unless the teachers are 'won over' to them, unless there is a change in their ideology. The prime needs are that they should both understand the reasons for and should be committed to the values of what is proposed, so that in-service back-up and every kind of support that is offered must be attuned to achieving both of these ends, and not merely to providing them with the new skills and techniques that will be required of them.

Summary and conclusions

We have considered in this opening chapter some definitions of the term 'curriculum', concluding that the most useful kind of definition we can adopt is one which is value-neutral and embraces all the planned activities of the school. We then looked at some of the points that have been made about the logic of curriculum planning and at some theoretical models that have been offered, noting in particular the suggestion that we should recognize the importance of the interplay between objectives, content, procedures and the data provided by evaluation processes in setting about planning a curriculum. We finally considered briefly some of the other factors that exercise their influence on curriculum planning, recognizing that this is not an activity that can profitably be regarded as going on, as it were, in a vacuum, but one which must be considered in its social context. This in turn led us to acknowledge the central role of the teacher in curriculum planning and development.

All of this suggests that we need to know more about how the curriculum changes, about the strategies of 'curriculum change' (Hoyle, 1969a,b), and that this is at least as important an area of exploration as, and perhaps even more important than, those considerations of a more theoretical kind about the logic of curriculum planning, about rational curriculum planning, that have hitherto tended to dominate the attention of curriculum theorists. Indeed, what is now happening is that we are being forced to recognize that curriculum development is a practical as much as, or more than, a theoretical activity and that here, as in all branches of the study of education, a linking of theory and practice is long overdue.

The main concern must be that teachers and all others who are involved in curriculum planning should be aware of all the factors involved. Curriculum development must be planned in such a way as to take full account of all relevant rational and logical considerations, but at the same time to take cognisance of those other pressures that are exerted directly and indirectly on such planning and to recognize those factors that are to be found within the situation for which the planning is being done. Only when these three elements have been considered together, balanced against each other and given their full weight in the planning process can we hope to achieve curriculum development that is rational, relevant and effective.

This in turn suggests that all curriculum development must be seen as essentially a matter of making modifications and adjustments to existing curricula in a way that makes full allowance for the idiosyncrasies of the individual situation and leads to evolution rather than revolution. Difficulties must arise if we regard curriculum development as a process of devising major innovations or projects and attempting to graft them on to living situations, the realities of which have not been taken into account in the planning of the project.

This would also suggest the need for a continuous study of curriculum issues of a kind that takes full account of the many facets of these issues that we have attempted to identify in this chapter. We must recognize that the study of the curriculum, again like the study of any other area of education, calls for a genuinely interdisciplinary and integrated approach. As should now be apparent, it is a field of study that draws on many sources of knowledge — on philosophy, logic and epistemology, on psychology, child development and theories of cognitive growth, on sociology both descriptive and phenomenological, on organizational theory and organizational studies, on history, on comparative studies and above all on an understanding of the practicalities of the real school situation in which any curriculum planning must be implemented.

Finally, in any exploration of the curriculum, we must remember the kind of theory we are dealing with. We have already noted the unavoidable value-element in curriculum planning and have suggested the impossibility of resolving this kind of question in any final, hard and fast way. Questions about the curriculum, like all questions in education, must remain open-ended and any answers we offer to them must be acknowledged as being tentative, hypothetical and subject to continuous review. Curriculum theory, therefore, must recognize that curriculum development must be a continuing process of evolution and planning. Knowledge continues to develop; society evolves; people change; and the curriculum must keep pace with all of these.

It is in this spirit that subsequent chapters in this book will consider some of the issues involved in those particular aspects of curriculum planning that the present chapter has endeavoured to isolate and to identify.

CHAPTER 2

CURRICULUM OBJECTIVES

We noted in Chapter 1 the claim that if curriculum planning is to be seen as a rational activity it must consist of at least three elements — choice of objectives, decisions about content, and selection of appropriate procedures. In practice these three elements will be inextricably interrelated with one another and in particular cases it will not be possible, at least without risk of serious distortion, to treat them separately. Indeed, it may well be that the most important area to be explored by curriculum theorists is the interrelationships between them. In looking at general problems of curriculum planning, however, if we are to achieve any real conceptual clarity, we must endeavour to separate them, to look at the particular difficulties associated with each in turn. It is the intention of this chapter to begin this process by considering some of the difficulties that surround discussions of curriculum objectives.

A concern with objectives has been one of the most striking features of the recent move towards deliberate curriculum planning which we also referred to in Chapter 1. It is not the case, of course, that educators were not concerned with objectives before this. It is probable that people have had aims and goals for any instruction or teaching they have engaged in almost from the beginning of time. Certainly many of the Greek and

Roman educationists display a concern with goals. From the beginning of the present century too, one can see, especially in the work of American educationists, a desire to examine questions of how educational objectives can best be specified (Popham 1969). It is also the case that for many years teachers and student-teachers have been expected by those responsible for supervising their work to begin the preparation of their lessons with statements of their objectives.

For a long time, however, little real attention was given to this issue of specifying objectives in curriculum planning, nor was it taken as a serious exercise by most teachers in planning their work. Perhaps this can be explained by the spread of the romantic view of education at the level of younger pupils with its reluctance to appear to interfere too extensively with their freedom and natural development and, conversely, an undue concern with subject content in the education of older pupils, in other words, the faults we suggested in Chapter 1 were associated with the 'progressive' and the 'traditional' approaches to curriculum planning. Whatever the reasons, little attention was given to the problems raised by the prespecification of curriculum objectives until recent times. Neither the publication in 1949 of Ralph Tyler's work which, as we noted in Chapter 1, offered a model of curriculum planning which commences with the specification of objectives nor, even more surprisingly, the publication by Benjamin Bloom and his associates in 1956 of what is still the most detailed and penetrating attempt at an analysis of educational objectives, the *Taxonomy of Educational Objectives*, had very much immediate impact on either the theory or the practice of curriculum planning.

Recently, however, this situation has changed and there has been revived a genuine interest in the problems involved in specifying educational objectives and a concern to pay due regard to them in curriculum planning, so that this has been the starting point, for example, for many curriculum projects developed under the aegis of the Schools Council.

At the same time, there are still those who positively eschew such an approach. The Humanities Curriculum Project, for example, has taken this line and, indeed, has suggested that prespecification of objectives is not appropriate within the humanities generally. Interdisciplinary Enquiry (IDE), as propounded by Goldsmiths' College Curriculum Laboratory, has also deliberately and consciously rejected an objectives approach (James 1968), regarding it as unsuitable to attempt to state in advance what the result of pupil enquiry should be.

Thus two points of view can be taken on this question, so that it is important for teachers and curriculum planners to be aware of the issues involved if they are to be able to decide on which approach is appropriate in their particular situation.

Prima facie, the arguments for the prespecification of objectives are strong. Some of them we touched upon in our discussion of curriculum models in Chapter 1. To begin with, it would seem to be a necessary part of any activity that is to be called rational that it should be geared towards some recognized purpose and should not be aimless or without direction. We have already referred to the criticism made of 'traditional' and 'progressive' curricula that both lack a proper recognition or identification of objectives and therefore, becoming obsessed with questions either of content or of procedures, fail to offer a proper perspective for rational curriculum planning. It would seem difficult to contradict the basic point that in planning a curriculum, as in any other rational activity, we should have some idea of where we are going and equally difficult to deny that it has been the lack of such a clear purpose that has constituted the main weakness in the practice of many schools, whether characterized as traditional or progressive. Where objectives are pre-specified, both teachers and pupils have a clear idea of what they are working towards so that it becomes possible for both to select and organize their work in the light of the criteria deriving from the stated goals of the activity.

A further and connected point emerges when we consider the fourth element in curriculum planning we identified in Chapter 1 — evaluation. For it is quite clear that evaluation will be much easier when one has stated in advance what one is hoping to achieve. Only then, perhaps, does one know with any degree of clarity what it is that is to be evaluated, since until one knows what outcomes were intended it might be felt that it is difficult to know how to assess what has been attained or achieved.

Why, then, have some people deliberately rejected this kind of approach to curriculum planning? The answer to this will perhaps begin to emerge if we look more closely at the nature of curriculum objectives and attempt to get a clearer view of what a curriculum objective is.

What is a curriculum objective?

We might begin this exploration by noting a generally accepted distinction between objectives and aims (Taba 1962). Aims are usually seen as very general statements of goals and purposes, such as to develop critical awareness or to promote understanding. Aims by themselves, however, have often been regarded as too general and lacking in specificity to provide clear guidelines for planners or teachers, so that curriculum planning has been seen as a process of developing more precise statements of goals from these general aims. It is these more precise statements that are normally termed objectives. Indeed, some writers have even suggested that we should recognize three or more levels of specificity (Kratwohl 1965) — general statements of goals that will guide the planning of the curriculum as a whole, behavioural objectives derived from these which will guide the planning of individual units or courses, and a third level of objectives appropriate in some cases to guide the planning of specific lessons, to use Wheeler's terms, 'ultimate', 'mediate' and 'proximate' goals, the latter providing specific classroom objectives (Wheeler 1967).

It is further argued that the quality of the instruction schools offer will continue to be low until we escape from our present wooly-mindedness and learn how to plan our work as teachers in this kind of detail. We must begin by stating clearly in advance the behavioural changes we are endeavouring to bring about. 'A satisfactory instructional objective must describe an observable *behaviour* of the learner or a *product* which is a consequence of learner behaviour' (Popham 1969, p. 35). The observable behaviour might take the form of something like 'skill in making impromptu speeches or performing gymnastic feats' (Popham 1969, p. 35). Products might be an essay or 'an omelet from the home economics class' (Popham 1969, p. 35).

This being so, 'a properly stated behavioural objective must describe *without ambiguity* the nature of learner behaviour or product to be measured' (Popham 1969, p. 37). For example:

> When given a description of a research design problem, the student can select correctly from the twenty statistical procedures treated in class that one which is most appropriate for analyzing the data to be produced by the research.

> Having been given a previously unencountered literary selection from nineteenth century English literature, the student will be able to write the name of the author and at least three valid reasons for making that selection (Popham 1969, p. 37).

Thus we are offered a hierarchy of goals, the main focus of which is the prespecification of behavioural objectives, 'intended learning outcomes' defined in terms of the kind of behaviour the pupil is intended or expected to display through his thoughts, actions or feelings if we are to be able to claim that our objective has been achieved.

The classic statement of this kind of hierarchy of goals is to be found in Bloom's taxonomy of educational objectives (Bloom et al. 1956; Kratwohl et al. 1964). The notion of the hierarchical nature of the inter-relationship of these objectives is fundamental to the taxonomy itself as is apparent from the gradation of objectives in the cognitive domain from the acquisition of the knowledge of specifics, through such higher level cognitive abilities as classification, comprehension, application, analysis, synthesis and so on to the making of evaluative judgements. Similar gradations are offered within each of the categories, comprehension, for example, being broken down into translation, interpretation and extrapolation.

However, Bloom also offers us another important distinction within this range of objectives since he divides them into three clear domains: the cognitive, the affective and the psychomotor — the head, the heart and the hand — the first two of which are fully worked out in the two volumes of the taxonomy. Thus he is suggesting that in framing our objectives we need to be clear not only about the sequential nature of the activity but also about the different categories of behaviour we might be concerned with. For the cognitive domain is defined as comprising 'objectives which emphasize remembering or reproducing something' which has presumably been learnt, as well as objectives which involve the solving of some intellective task for which the individual has to determine the essential problem and then reorder given material or combine it with ideas, methods or procedures previously learned' (Kratwohl et al. 1964, p. 6). The affective domain, we are told, comprises 'objectives which emphasize a feeling tone, an emotion, or a degree of acceptance or rejection' (Kratwohl et al. 1964, p. 7). Finally, the psycho-motor domain consists of 'objectives which emphasize some muscular or motor skill, some manipulation of material and objects, or some act which requires a neuromuscular coordination' (Kratwohl et al. 1964, p. 7).

Thus these two dimensions Bloom and his associates offer us enable us to prespecify our objectives at varying levels of specificity in order to outline in great detail the kinds of behaviour which are the objectives of our curriculum. It is easy to see why this approach has proved so attractive to some curriculum planners.

Conversely, however, it is when we are offered this kind of highly detailed statement of how a curriculum is to be planned in terms of objectives that we begin to see what it is that other people have found unacceptable in this approach, or at least we begin to become aware that it is not such a straightforward matter as it may at first have appeared to be.

The results of Bloom's work, therefore, have been twofold. On the one hand, recent years have seen a proliferation of curriculum projects which have begun diligently with detailed statements of their objectives; on the other hand, we have also witnessed a developing movement away from the idea of prespecified curriculum objectives, a reaction against what has begun to appear to some as an undue limitation on the scope of the teacher as an educator.

A good example of the former would be the elaborate table of objectives given by the Schools Council's Science 5-13 project team (Schools Council 1972) which begins by listing nine broad aims focused on the central goal of developing an enquiring mind and a scientific approach to problems and then proceeds to break these broad aims down into a detailed list of shorter-term behavioural objectives, grouped in such a way as to be closely linked to the children's stages of conceptual development. Thus at the second part of Stage 1, the early stage of concrete operations, the broad aim of developing interests, attitudes and aesthetic awareness is broken down into four objectives:

Desire to find out things for oneself

Willing participation in group work

Willing compliance with safety regulations in handling tools and equipment

Appreciation of the need to learn the meaning of new words and to use them correctly

(Schools Council 1972a, p. 60).

Another example is the statement of the objectives of the teaching of home economics as outlined in Schools Council Curriculum Bulletin No. 4. These are given under the general headings, Development of personal qualities, Intellectual development, Discrimination and aesthetic appreciation, The needs of the adolescent, Future needs, Skills and knowledge, and they include such things as 'to develop a sense of responsibility and service towards other pupils and towards the home and school communities', 'to cultivate an intelligent attitude towards home-making, including the social, financial, nutritional and practical aspects', 'to develop recognition and appreciation of craftsmanship, quality and good design', 'to encourage the constructive use of leisure time', 'to give the girls an awareness of their potential as women, wives and mothers of the future', 'to teach pupils to understand the topics which we consider most important, e.g. basic nutrition, budgeting, hygiene, home safety', 'to encourage enjoyment of the subject and the development of particular interests and talents', 'to train girls to act sensibly in an emergency' (Schools Council 1971b, pp. 9/10).

Even the most cursory reading of these examples drawn from the stated objectives of one area of the curriculum will make immediately apparent some of the difficulties that have been identified in this kind of approach to curriculum planning and will explain why other projects, notably the Humanities Curriculum Project and the more recent Bruner-sponsored project, Man A Course of Study (MACOS), have deliberately eschewed the idea of prespecifying their objectives. We must now, therefore, look in rather more detail at some of the problems inherent in this approach to curriculum planning.

Some criticisms of Bloom's taxonomy

The two main criticisms that have been levelled at the taxonomy of Bloom have been, firstly, that it sets out to be far too precise and specific and, secondly, that it lacks a clear concept of education and, as a result, offers us no criteria for the evaluation of objectives, no basis upon which we might make a choice of what are the most appropriate objectives in a given context. Let us consider these two criticisms in turn.

There are obvious attractions in the idea of a fairly precise prespecification of objectives and these attractions derive not least, as we have seen, from the fact that they lead to a relative ease of evaluation procedures. The more clearly we state our goals the easier it will be to assess whether we have attained them or not, although teachers have been aware for some time of the dangers of allowing evaluation procedures to rule their curriculum planning, in particular the danger of restricting themselves to those activities which lend themselves most readily to the forms of assessment available to them — a problem that may be inherent in any approach that sees all objectives as behavioural objectives.

However, the main point of the criticism that this approach is too precise and specific derives from the fact that in practice, and perhaps at a theoretical level too, it is not possible to distinguish objectives in such a detailed way. Every activity in which a pupil engages will have a range of objectives both within and between the three 'domains'. This is brought out very well in the general statement of the traditional objectives of craft teaching offered by the architects of the Schools Council's project, 'Education through the use of materials', as 'developing motor skills, such as sawing, planing and filing, and appreciation of design and craftsmanship in furniture and engineering, with all the satisfaction that attainment in these activities can bring to some pupils and which for so long have been the "bread and butter" activity of the workshop'. (Schools Council 1969a, p. 10.) It is also well illustrated by the assertion already referred to that one objective of the teaching of home economics should be 'to encourage enjoyment of the subject and the development of particular interests and talents'. The Science 5-13 project too has stated quite clearly that 'a teacher will have many objectives for her children in mind at any one time, and in general there is potential for working towards several objectives through any one activity (Schools Council 1972a, p. 32). At one level this may seem to amount to no more than saying that in practice every activity will embody a range of objectives, involving 'some intellective task', 'a degree of acceptance or rejection' and probably 'some manipulation of materials and objects' too.

At a deeper level, however, it might be claimed that what this implies is rather more than a gap between theory and practice, since it draws attention to a fundamental feature of education, namely that it does violence to the notion of education to suggest that even at a theoretical level the development of knowledge and skills of any kind can be divorced from the simultaneous promotion of a feeling for standards of truth and beauty which are part of what it means to have knowledge and to be educated (Pring 1971). It has been argued, therefore, that not only in practice but also at the conceptual level objectives are much too closely interrelated to be capable of being developed into this particular kind of detailed hierarchical taxonomy that Bloom is offering.

To look at this from a different point of view and in more detail, the real thrust of this criticism is that the relationship that exists between educational objectives is too complex to be reduced to an unsophisticated model of this kind which sees that relationship as a hierarchy of simple to ever more complex objectives (Hirst 1975). The relationships existing between the many things that teachers are endeavouring to achieve with their pupils are far more complicated than such a model supposes. Furthermore, such a model assumes that all educational objectives are behavioural objectives, attempts to modify or change the behaviour of pupils, the results of which can be readily assessed by observation of pupil behaviour and, although some statements of objectives, such as those we have already referred to, are framed in such a way as to make such an assumption not unreasonable, a moment's observation of any teacher's classroom practice will reveal that not only are the relationships between objectives highly complex, but the objectives themselves are too varied and sophisticated to be reduced to one type or category. This is a point we must take up later.

Lastly, we should note that little practical help is given in the matter of curriculum planning by a taxonomy which offers us only general categories of objective. We need to know more about the relationships existing between particular sets of objectives in the individual context in which we happen to be working. Such a taxonomy assumes that the only factor to be taken account of in the framing of objectives is that of the logical relationships between them. In the reality of any practical situation the logic of our objectives is only one consideration that we must keep in mind. The actual planning of any piece of work will require that we take full account of many other factors of a psychological, sociological and educational kind (Hirst 1975).

In short, Bloom's taxonomy, in being very precise, takes too naive a view of educational processes and thus provides an over-simplified model for curriculum planning which must inevitably, if pursued too slavishly, lead to bad educational practice.

This is one aspect of a greater weakness in the taxonomy, namely that it gives no account of the view of the nature of knowledge on which it is grounded; it has no clearly worked-out epistemological basis (Pring 1971). Such a basis would seem to be an essential prerequisite for any taxonomy of educational objectives, since, whatever else education is concerned with, it is certainly concerned with cognitive development of many kinds, with the acquisition of knowledge of many forms. We have already noted one result of this lack, namely the difficulties it creates when one tries to isolate the affective from the cognitive domain. The second problem that it raises is more germane to our present discussion, since, in making distinctions within the cognitive domain like those between knowledge and other intellectual abilities such as comprehension, application, analysis, and so on, the taxonomy again fails to recognize the interrelatedness of these intellectual abilities. As has been pointed out (Pring 1971) it does not make sense to attempt to bring children to know and then to comprehend and then to apply their knowledge. Understanding is not something we aim at after knowledge has been acquired but something we seek simultaneously with its acquisition. Even the most elementary examination of what knowledge is would reveal this, as would the most superficial consideration of what education is.

This leads us on naturally to an examination of the other major criticism that has been levelled at Bloom's taxonomy, namely that it lacks any concept of education and, therefore, provides no basis for the selection of objectives or the evaluation of one against another (Gribble 1970). The taxonomy is deliberately neutral and offers no criteria by which we can decide what will count as an *educational* objective. It might be argued that any hierarchy must be based on some system of values, that no hierarchy can be value-neutral. but, as we have just seen, this particular hierarchical structure endeavours to avoid issues of value by basing itself solely on the considerations of which objectives are logically prior and prerequisite to others and perhaps the psychological consideration of which simple objectives must have been achieved before children can be taken on to the more complex ones. To emphasize this feature is to start from the assumption that one's job is merely to describe the kinds of objective teachers can be seen to be pursuing, 'school' objectives rather than 'educational' objectives, and the logical and psychological factors that suggest that to be effective they should be tackled in a certain sequence. It does not commit itself on the question of whether such objectives *should* be pursued by teachers, or whether they are part of what we mean by 'education'.

This is an inevitable feature not only of Bloom's taxonomy but of any behavioural objectives model of curriculum planning. For by seeing education as the changing of behaviour this model attempts to avoid such questions as the directions in which it is desirable to change pupils' behaviour or what kinds of behaviour are worth promoting and leaves those issues to the person using the model (Sockett 1976). The result is that teachers and other curriculum planners are offered no grounds on which to evaluate competing claims against one another — the problem we saw in Chapter 1 to be crucial to curriculum planning — nor any grounds upon which to evaluate the suitability of their objectives either before or during or after a particular project or piece of work.

Again the result of these weaknesses in the taxonomy will be difficulties or even dangers for anyone attempting to use it in a practical situation. It will be either misleading or useless. Furthermore, the failure of this attempt at setting up a taxonomy of educational objectives as a basis for rational curriculum planning must cast doubt on this approach to curriculum planning in general, not least because, as we have just seen, some of the criticisms made of it will apply equally to any scheme that begins by specifying behavioural objectives and proceeds to plan those activities and experiences that appear most likely to lead to the attainment of these objectives. In short, it must lead us to question the validity of this kind of model of curriculum planning.

A number of people have, therefore, rejected the whole approach to curriculum planning through the prespecification of objectives and we must now turn to an examination of some of their more cogent reasons for doing so.

Curriculum planning without prespecified objectives

The first points that must be made in listing reasons why many people reject this approach to curriculum planning are those that derive from practical considerations. In the first place, there are a good many difficulties in measuring the attainment of behavioural objectives. What sorts of evidence would constitute proof of the fact that we have brought about the behaviour changes we have been striving for? Pupils can very easily 'go through the motions' they know we require of them and it is very difficult, if not impossible, to distinguish with any degree of accuracy occasions when this is happening from those when a genuine behavioural change has been brought about. Such an approach, therefore, perhaps invites the generation of 'inert ideas' (Whitehead 1932) or at least makes it difficult for us to ensure that real understanding is achieved.

A second issue that we must not ignore at the level of the practicalities of curriculum planning is that, while the theorists argue the case for or against the prespecification of curriculum objectives, the teachers themselves in planning their courses seldom begin from this standpoint but from considerations of a much more practical and mundane kind (Taylor 1970). We mentioned earlier in this chapter that for many years the notion of curriculum objectives was slow to gain hold even at the level of curriculum theory. It has still failed to establish itself in the practice of most teachers.

As we suggested earlier, teachers and student-teachers have for a long time engaged in the game of stating the objectives of their lessons when this has been required of them by inspectors, head teachers or college tutors. To a large extent, however, the main result of this has been to establish at least to their own satisfaction how fatuous an exercise this can be, so that they have learnt from it not to plan their work in this way but rather to reject this approach as having little direct bearing on their practice, since the realities of any teacher's lessons will always have only the loosest links with any objectives he may have set himself in advance.

It may be that they have thus come to realize, long before the curriculum theorists got onto it, that to state one's objectives in advance in terms of intended behavioural changes and to stick rigidly to such a plan or programme is to fail to take account of the complexities of the curriculum and of the importance of the individual context in which every act of teaching occurs (Sockett 1976).

One major reason, then, why some people have recently wished to argue against the prespecification of objectives is the conviction that education is a more sophisticated activity and curriculum planning as a result a more complex process than this simple theoretical model suggests. This is a point we have noted several times already. In Chapter 1, for example, we suggested that the model of curriculum planning as a straight linear progression from prespecification of objectives *via* decisions about suitable content and procedures to evaluation of intended learning outcomes is far too unsophisticated and inadequate for the planning of any educational activity. We suggested then that the continuous interaction of all the elements involved in curriculum planning was important and had to be allowed for by the adoption of a model that was at the very least cyclical, resulting in modifications of our objectives in the light of the evaluations made, or, preferably, one that allowed for constant modification of objectives in the light of continuous evaluation.

We must note now that this latter kind of model accords more closely with the practice of teachers in most kinds of educational situation. Sensitive teachers do make constant adjustments to their procedures and to their objectives in the light of the continuous feedback they get from their pupils as any piece of work progresses. This is true even of those teachers who do begin by setting out their terminal objectives very precisely. We have already noted too that factors other than prestated objectives will influence their decisions about content and procedures and these factors in turn will also result in modifications to these objectives.

Furthermore, we must recognize that, as we have just suggested, all such modifications will be made according to the individual teacher's interpretation of the values implicit in the originally prespecified objectives (Stenhouse 1970) and his own reaction to the response of the pupils to the work and any other factors which he regards as relevant. In short, they will be made in relation to the individual context of each teacher's work. It is for this reason that the results of any educational programme will always differ from the expectations of its planners (Stenhouse 1970) and this is one factor in the recent move towards seeing curriculum development as essentially a matter of local development within a particular school rather than in terms of the generation of projects to be disseminated nationally.

Any model we adopt for curriculum planning must allow for the personal and professional autonomy of the teacher, especially in relation to the framing and modification of objectives, as the experience of a number of curriculum projects, such as the Schools Council project on History, Geography and Social Science 8-13, has revealed (Blyth 1974). If we do not allow for this, then we create constraints on the activity of teachers and their scope for exercising their professional judgement on the spot. This is clearly a very real danger with too simple an objectives model.

This approach also creates similar constraints on the freedom of pupils. As Charity James has argued (James 1968), both teachers and pupils tend to accept objectives as in some sense 'given' and unquestionable and thus both lose the opportunity to be active participants in the educational process. Thus it is argued that the prespecification of intended learning outcomes to an educational process denies autonomy not only to the teacher but also to the pupil and anything that does not take account of the incipient and developing autonomy of the pupil cannot be accurately described as educative (Pring 1973). If education is seen as a continuous, ongoing, open-ended activity, then the idea of constant modification and reassessment must be endemic to it, so that any approach to the planning of an educational activity that starts with a clear specification of objectives will be based on a misunderstanding of what an educational activity really is.

This point, of course, raises some much more fundamental theoretical issues concerning the nature of education and, indeed, the nature of man. To place this kind of emphasis on the developing autonomy of the individual is to make certain profound assumptions both about what education is and about the sort of being man is. For to see the activities that the teacher plans for his pupils in terms of closely specifiable learning outcomes is to take a totally behaviourist view of human psychology and to adopt a passive model of man, seeing all or most of human behaviour as explicable in terms of causes rather than purposes. In other words, it regards the teacher's task as being to condition pupils into certain kinds of behaviour and in doing so it does not allow that man is an active creature some of whose behaviour must be seen as the result of those purposes that he frames for himself as an autonomous thinking being and who requires, therefore, not to be conditioned into certain kinds of response to certain kinds of stimuli, but to be educated to think for himself and to frame his own purposes for his own autonomous behaviour. If one takes this view of man as active rather than passive, and of man's behaviour as explicable in terms of reasons and purposes as well as in causal terms, then one must accept that there is a vital distinction between education and conditioning or training and, therefore, some consequential difficulties for the statement of educational goals in terms of behavioural objectives.

In fact, there arises a further conceptual problem from this very notion of educational goals. For it has been claimed that one of the things that characterizes education as opposed to other activities that involve teaching and learning, such as training or instruction, is that education is essentially concerned with activities whose value is intrinsic to them (Peters 1965). Such a notion of education as consisting of certain activities that are regarded as intrinsically worthwhile is clearly at odds with the idea of activities planned according to extrinsic behavioural objectives, goals extrinsic to the activity itself. It was John Dewey who first drew our attention to this feature of education when he asserted that education can have no ends beyond itself, since it is its own end. This view has subsequently been developed more fully by Richard Peters (Peters 1965, 1966, 1973a) who claims, for example, that 'to be educated is not to have arrived at a destination; it is to travel with a different view. What is required is not feverish preparation for something that lies ahead, but to work with precision, passion and taste at worthwhile things that lie at hand' (Peters 1965, p. 110). On this kind of analysis not only does the notion of prespecified behavioural objectives run counter to the very concept of education but the broad aims of education must also be seen from a different perspective, not as what education is *for* but as what it *is*, so that to assert that education is concerned with the development of personal autonomy, understanding, a cognitive perspective, a recognition of the value of certain kinds of activity and so on is not to state extrinsic goals for education so much as to identify features that should characterize any process that is to be described as educational. This is a point we must take up again later.

On this kind of argument what is fundamentally wrong with Bloom's approach and, indeed, with any approach to the planning of a curriculum that begins from a careful and detailed prespecification of objectives is that it adopts an overtly means/end view which causes us to lose sight of a basic principle of education. One further important aspect of this is that it reduces the role of the content of our curriculum to an instrumental one (Stenhouse 1970), thus introducing a utilitarian element into the pupil's view of what he is being encouraged to learn, with all the unsatisfactory consequences of that (MacIntyre 1964). For in a wider sense, it was this feature of the traditional view of education, derived from Plato and adopted uncritically within Christian educational theory, as a means to the achievement of extrinsic ends, as an instrumental process, that led to many of the inadequacies of educational practice with which we are familiar and invited the reaction against it that is sometimes, and perhaps misleadingly, described as 'progressive education'. The traditional view saw the child as a 'man in the making' and the aims of education as statements about the sort of man education should be concerned to make — whether the obedient citizen or the cultured gentleman or the philosopher king. The reaction against this began with Rousseau's demand that we view and treat the child as a child and let him grow naturally. Whatever the difficulties of this counter view — and they are many — it has the merit of drawing our attention to the danger of taking an instrumental view of education and of seeing the content of our curriculum purely in terms of its suitability for the attainment of certain goals, a feature of Plato's theory of education that has perhaps not been hitherto sufficiently recognized.

The third major difficulty of the objectives approach to curriculum planning follows naturally from this. Once we adopt a model that allows us to see content as instrumental, we immediately risk slipping into some kind of indoctrinatory process, as an examination of Plato's theory of education will again quickly reveal. For there are many areas of the curriculum which involve content of a kind which is highly controversial and to approach these areas with a clear prespecification of intended learning outcomes in behavioural terms is to abandon education altogether for what must be seen as a much more sinister process. In the teaching and learning of music and the fine arts the prime concern is to elicit an individual response from the pupil; it is clearly not appropriate to decide in advance what that response should be (Eisner 1969). 'How can you put on the blackboard the mysterious internal goal of each creative person?' (Pirsig 1974). In literature too the whole purpose of introducing pupils to great literary works is lost if it is done from the perspective of intended learning outcomes (Stenhouse 1970). Again that purpose is to invite the pupil to respond in his own way to what he is introduced to. To approach a reading of *Hamlet*, for example, in any other way is either to reduce it to an instrumental role, as we have just seen, designed to promote an understanding of words, poetic forms, even philosophy, or to attempt to impose one's own subjective interpretation of the play and response to it on one's pupils. If appreciation of literature or any of the arts means anything at all and has any place in education, it cannot be approached by way of clearly prespecified objectives.

This is one of the major reasons why the Schools Council's Humanities Curriculum Project has deliberately eschewed any kind of statement of objectives and, indeed, has gone so far as to make teacher neutrality its central principle. Being concerned to introduce older pupils in secondary schools to some of the controversial issues that face modern society, issues like those of relations between the sexes, race relations, war and so on, and being aware that these are issues upon which a number of different value stances can be taken with equal validity, it has recognized that the involvement of pupils in these issues cannot be undertaken justifiably with clear objectives as to what the outcome of their learning and discussions should be, but only according to certain procedural principles that will allow them to reach their own informed opinions on them. To do anything else would be to indoctrinate rather than to educate.

For some areas of the curriculum, then, certainly for those areas that comprise the expressive arts and the humanities, there is this further strong argument against planning in terms of prespecified objectives. Indeed, it may well not be limited to the expressive arts and the humanities. Certainly there is a similar argument that can be adduced for the teaching of science. For it might be argued that even in the sciences to prespecify the outcome of an experiment, for example, is to go against one of the fundamental principles of scientific method, namely that every scientific hypothesis is problematic and subject to modification or even rejection, so that whatever evidence an experiment produces must be seriously evaluated against currently accepted hypotheses (Sockett 1976). If we are really concerned as teachers of science to get our pupils to think scientifically, therefore, we will not begin by asserting what the results of their experiments should be; we will let them evaluate the results of their own experimentation for themselves.

Again we are reminded of the point we have made several times — that this is all a result of being too ready to accept as our main tasks as teachers those things that can be easily prespecified and therefore equally easily evaluated. Curriculum development must involve much more than just those things. If it does not then it will be a very 'blinkered' activity.

We are thus faced by a dilemma. On the one hand, it would seem that all rational activities must be characterized as having clear purposes and intentions; on the other hand, if what we plan for our pupils in schools has such clear purposes and intentions, it is likely to fall short of being educational in' the full sense and may even appear to be something sinister. What then is the solution?

Alternative models of curriculum objectives

The first point to be made in answer to this question is that there ought not to be any fundamental contradiction between the idea of rational curriculum planning and that of promoting the process of education. In other words, the fact that we are faced with this dilemma is more likely to suggest that our thinking has gone wrong somewhere than that a real impasse exists. For this reason it has been suggested that it is not the specification of objectives in itself which causes the troubles we have listed but rather a misunderstanding as to the kind of thing an educational objective is (Hirst 1975). In short, it is said that we must look for another model for curriculum objectives, since the behavioural model of curriculum objectives is unsatisfactory. Firstly, it is unsatisfactory precisely because it is behavioural and, therefore, loses sight of the fact that educational objectives must of their very nature be concerned with much more complex forms of 'personal and mental development (Hirst 1975, p. 15). Secondly, it is based on a misunderstanding of the relationship between objectives. Thirdly, it leads to a view of curriculum planning as a kind of engineering or computer-programming which fails to understand how curriculum objectives come to be framed. Lastly, it operates at too general a level, assuming that curricula can be planned in a Utopian, *carte blanche* manner rather than recognizing that curriculum development must be seen as a piecemeal activity taking place in specific contexts (Hirst 1975).

It is not the idea of having a purpose to our planning that is at fault. It is the way in which we view that purpose and its relations to the activities that will embody it. Given that the engineering or computer-programming model is inadequate and accepting that a horticultural model of largely undirected growth of the kind that Rousseau seemed to advocate is equally unsatisfactory, we must set about the search for a more suitable model rather than reject the idea of specifying objectives altogether.

On the other hand, it is difficult to know what an educational objective would be if it were not to be seen as a statement of the intention to change or modify behaviour, unless it were a general statement of principle, a long-term aim. Any short-term goal must be expressed in terms of the behaviour changes we hope to bring about. Certainly the only way in which we could measure the achievement of a short-term goal would be by examining the behaviour of our pupils. Thus, even if we attempted to express the goals of a lesson in terms of *educational* objectives, such as 'to develop habits of enquiry', rather than tight *behavioural* objectives or 'intended learning outcomes', our intention would still be to change behaviour and our success of failure must still be evaluated by observation of pupil behaviour. Any short-term goal, therefore, must be behavioural in nature, although this does not need to be interpreted from the perspective of the behavioural psychologist.

It is for this reason that we are now being encouraged from a number of sources to adopt a much looser approach to the framing of objectives so as to avoid a tight computer-programming approach to pupil activities. It has been suggested, for example, that we do begin by stating course objectives but that we avoid the temptation to frame them in highly specific behavioural terms (Hogben 1972) and that we should not be afraid to state long-term objectives, since many important educational outcomes may not be achieved except after many months or years of effort (Hogben 1972). It is further suggested that we be on the alert for unexpected or unintended outcomes (Hogben 1972, p. 48) and that we do not reject or discourage these merely because they do not conform to our prestated short-term goals. In short, we should regard our objectives, certainly those of a short-term variety, as provisional, 'mutable and subject to modification in the light of the continuous experience both of ourselves as teachers and of our pupils once a course or piece of work has got under way. This continuous adaptation to new data is after all a perfectly normal feature of most or all rational activities including that which has often been regarded as the paradigm of such activity, scientific exploration. Only thus can curriculum planning properly become curriculum *development*. This was the experience, for example, of those working on the Schools Council Project on History, Geography and Social Science 8—13, to which we have already referred, which found that in order to allow for the autonomy of both teachers and pupils the objectives framed for both had to be regarded as provisional and open to constant reinterpretation (Blyth 1974). For the same reason, the planners of the Nuffield 'A' level biological science project introduced the notion of 'mutable' objectives (Kelly, P. J. 1973). In short, 'objectives are developmental, representing roads to travel rather than terminal points' (Taba 1962, p. 203). Another way of putting this would be to say that the objectives model is useful but has its limitations or that at least its role in curriculum planning has been overstated (Stenhouse 1970).

It is from similar considerations that Elliot Eisner has suggested that we make a distinction between instructional and expressive objectives (Eisner 1969). An expressive objective does not specify an outcome of instruction in behavioural terms. 'An expressive objective describes an educational encounter. It identifies a situation in which children are to work, a problem with which they are to cope, a task in which they are to engage; but it does not specify what from that encounter, situation, problem, or task they are to learn. . . . An expressive objective is evocative rather than prescriptive' (Eisner 1969, pp. 15—16).

He gives as examples of expressive objectives:

1)   To interpret the meaning of *Paradise Lost*,

2)   To examine and appraise the significance of *The Old Man and the Sea*,

3)   To develop a three-dimensional form through the use of wire and wood,

4)   To visit the zoo and discuss what was of interest there.

(Eisner 1969, p. 16.)

He goes on to suggest further that it is this kind of objective that teachers have more often than they have instructional objectives of a behavioural kind and that this is particularly so in 'the most sophisticated modes of intellectual work' (Eisner 1969, p. 17). This is a point we must take up later. It is sufficient if we note here that to use the term 'objective' to signify this kind of approach to educational planning is slightly odd and misleading, since it is to use a term with connotations of extrinsic goals to denote a notion the essence of which seems to be a concern with processes.

It is as a result of this kind of consideration, therefore, that others have gone further and advised that we turn from this search for objectives of any kind and devote our attention instead to achieving agreement on the broad principles that are to inform the activity or course we are planning and in the light of which all on-the-spot decisions and modifications will be made.

Lawrence Stenhouse, for example, has suggested that 'in mounting curriculum research and development, we shall in general . . . do better to deal in hypotheses concerning effects than in objectives. To attach the value-laden tag, *objectives*, to some of our hypotheses is an odd and usually unproductive scientific procedure' (Stenhouse 1970, p. 80). Such an approach, he is claiming, will encourage us to be much more tentative, less dogmatic and more aware of the possibility of failure and the need for corrective adjustments than statements of objectives which may lead us to feel we know where we are going without fear of contradiction. He has also suggested that we should begin by defining the 'value positions embodied in the curriculum specification or specifications' (Stenhouse 1970, p. 82). Again, to do this will provide us with a clear view of the principles upon which the original planning was founded which can act as a basis either for later changes in our procedures or for modification of these value positions themselves in the light of subsequent experience.

This is a point that Richard Pring has taken up in urging teachers and curriculum planners to seek for agreement on the principles of procedure that will guide the conduct of any particular curriculum project and to concern themselves not with prespecifying goals but with statements of the norms and principles that will inform the activity of both teachers and pupils (Pring 1973). Only thus, it is argued, will it be possible for us to reconcile the idea of rational curriculum planning with that of education as a continuous life-long process to which terminal goals cannot be attributed.

It was on this kind of base that the Schools Council's Humanities Curriculum Project was established, making no attempt to specify learning outcomes but stating quite clearly the principles to be adhered to in the classroom. In fact this has been the practice of most curriculum projects. For where objectives are stated, these are seldom really short-term, but usually have a kind of 'middle-ground' appearance and are stated in general procedural terms. In other words, they are often neither very broad educational aims nor immediate intended outcomes but rather statements of the general principles that the project team felt should underlie the work of a particular subject area. If they are to be called objectives at all, they resemble Eisner's expressive objectives rather than instructional objectives framed in behavioural terms.

This is the only interpretation that can be put on a statement of objectives such as that of the Schools Council Working Paper No. 24 — *Rural Studies in Secondary Schools*, which set out the following five objectives:

a)   To promote an understanding of the countryside and man's relation to his natural environment and to develop a respect for living things

b)   To develop an understanding of science and scientific method through observation, first-hand investigation, and experiment

c)   To give enjoyment and satisfaction, and to encourage a profitable use of leisure

d)   To develop aesthetic appreciation and an outlet for creative thinking

e)   To arouse the interest of all pupils through acceptable and enjoyable practical work, and in this manner to provide valuable starting points for further studies.

(Schools Council 1969b, pp. 9—10.)

Such a statement clearly does not offer a programme of behavioural objectives but it does provide a set of guidelines for teachers to refer to in the planning of their own particular programmes or the work of individual pupils.

What has happened seems to be that people are very confused in their thinking about objectives, so that they call what they are doing framing objectives but then proceed to make these of such a general kind that they are not objectives in the instructional and behavioural sense of the term at all, but rather expressive objectives or principles of the kind we have been discussing. Thus even the Schools Council's Science 5—13 project which sets out a programme of objectives with a very 'taxonomous' look to it is at pains at the same time to stress that all of these objectives are at a level of generality such as to give both teachers and children a good deal of freedom over choices of activity, materials, experiments and so on (Schools Council 1972a). Indeed, the experience of that project points up precisely the problem we have been endeavouring to air, since its objectives could not be tightly framed without being in conflict with the enquiry approach to science that it was also at pains to promote.

Most people do seem in fact to accept that an educational curriculum must be viewed in terms of processes rather than content or behavioural outcomes. One might express this by saying with Richard Peters that it is the manner rather than the matter of learning that we must look to in defining an educational activity (Peters 1965). Or one might claim with Paul Hirst that to be initiated into the several forms of thought is more important than to acquire the ability merely to perform certain intellectual feats (Hirst 1965), the ability to think scientifically, for example, being what the notion of education requires rather than the mere display of certain behaviours recognizable as regurgitating statements of scientific 'fact . Or one might argue with Alfred North Whitehead that education is 'the art of the utilization of knowledge' and not the acquisition of 'inert ideas' (Whitehead 1932). Again one might accept John Dewey's claim that all knowledge is to be seen as the developing experience of the individual. One might even take the line of those sociologists who argue that education, to be meaningful to the pupil, must be a development of the knowledge he brings to the school with him (Keddie 1971).

It all comes down to the same thing fundamentally, namely that education and, therefore, the curriculum has to be planned in the light of those processes it is seen to comprise rather than in terms either of the subject content it is claimed it should contain or include or a set of behavioural outcomes it is designed to promote or achieve. Aims and processes cannot be separated; the aims are reflected in the processes and the processes are embodied in the aims.

The difficulty arises when the framing of short-term goals is seen as a tight deductive process from these broader statements of aims, processes or principles. It is the relation of our short-term objectives to these longer-term aims that is the crucial issue. The model that is unacceptable for all the reasons we have listed at length is that which offers us a hierarchy of goals, beginning, for example, with the *ultimate* goals of all education, deriving from these *mediate* goals for different stages of learning, deducing from these *proximate* goals for shorter-term activities and finally drawing from these specific classroom *objectives* (Wheeler 1967). It is infinitely preferable that after agreement has been reached at the level of general principles, teachers and pupils should be given the autonomy to interpret these principles in their own way in the planning of their varied and continuing activities. In practice, this seems to be what most projects in the last analysis do anyway, so that once again it seems that we have a problem created for us by the theorists. There are, of course, dangers here that teachers and pupils will either fail to use or will misuse their autonomy (Blyth 1974) but unless this risk is taken and they are given this freedom, nothing that can be characterized as education is likely to take place and no curriculum *development* will be possible. This looser model is the only acceptable model for both the rational planning and the continuous development of an educational curriculum.

This brings us to a final point which must be noted here, although it has already been referred to. It may well be that we need to seek different solutions to this dilemma over objectives in considering different areas of the curriculum or the work of different age-ranges, although, as we suggested earlier, it may equally well be the case that at a fundamental level no such differences should exist. Certainly, however, we should note here the difference between education and schooling and recognize that the problems we have been discussing relate to the planning of *educational* activities in terms of prespecified goals.

Education, however, is not the only process that involves teaching and/or learning, nor is it the only thing that schools are responsible for and need therefore to plan. Schools are also responsible for a good deal of training and the teaching of physical skills, sometimes as a preliminary to some educational activity but sometimes, as with some vocational training or games coaching, as a totally separate activity; they also concern themselves with such things as socialization and other activities whose goals are clearly specifiable. A tight behavioural objectives model might be the right model for the planning of programmes of work in these areas and we should not allow what has been said about the unsuitability of such a model for the planning of educational activities to cause us to abandon it for all purposes.

Indeed, this may point us towards what begins to seem to be a fundamental feature of educational objectives, namely that in some strange way they are concerned with means rather than with ends. If they have any place in the educational process at all, it is as statements of immediate and short-term pieces of learning that are to be undertaken, skills to be attained or facts to be acquired as staging posts on the road to the achievement of an education which can itself be defined only in terms of broad principles and not in terms of specific and prespecifiable behavioural changes.

It is precisely, therefore, because many people feel that there is much more to schooling than can be expressed in terms of such short-term objectives and are committed to the view of education and of the nature of man we discussed earlier, that we have directed our main attention to what that entails for curriculum planning.

Sources of procedural principles

We have argued that the only way in which we can make sense of the idea of objectives within a context of educational activities is to view them as procedural principles rather than terminal goals, to direct our attention to processes rather than aims. We must now consider briefly the question of where such principles will derive from or of the kinds of consideration upon which they might be framed. We saw when criticizing Bloom's taxonomy that it was at fault not only in its too precise specification of learning outcomes but also in being value-neutral, in merely describing what teachers do rather than attempting to evaluate what they do and to suggest what they ought to be doing. We said then that if we profess to be concerned with *educational* objectives, we need some concept of education in the light of which we can decide which objectives are to count as educational. The same must be true of any statement of the procedural principles that are to inform our curriculum. These cannot be merely plucked out of the air nor made up in an 'off-the-cuff' manner. They must be firmly rooted in a concept of what constitutes an educational activity.

A lot will hinge, therefore, on the view one takes of education. This would appear perhaps on the surface to open up the whole issue to the subjective judgements of individuals and to raise all the problems of values that we referred to in Chapter 1 and will consider again in Chapter 3. However, at the level of ultimate educational principles the situation is unlikely to be as open as this. For, as we have seen, to be faced with this problem in the first place implies that one is committed to a view of education as quite different from those activities that can be defined in means/end terms; in other words that one has a concept of education as an activity distinct from training, indoctrination, socialization and so on. This in turn will imply a view of education, such as that so thoroughly analysed and explicated by Richard Peters (Peters 1965, 1966, 1973a), as an activity characterized by such general features as the intrinsic value and valuing of its content. the development of understanding or a true cognitive perspective rather than the mere acquisition of knowledge, a respect for standards of truth and the promotion of individual autonomy. To recognize that problems exist over the planning of educational activities in terms of clear objectives or intended learning outcomes is in itself to be committed to a view of education as embodying these principles, and these principles are surely enough to be going on with.

It is in the interpretation of such principles in terms of specific activities, subject content or shorter-term goals that the difficulties arise, as we suggested earlier. It is clear that what happens in practice is that those concerned with curriculum planning at different levels each make their own interpretations, albeit in interaction with each other. Thus a project team will formulate provisional objectives after a detailed analysis of the area of the curriculum with which it is concerned and usually in dialogue with educationists in Colleges and Departments of Education and with teachers concerned with the area (Blyth 1974). The statement of objectives for Rural Studies given in the Schools Council's Working Paper No. 24, for example, which we have already quoted, was reached in part as a result of a survey of the schools teaching the subject and of the aims they acknowledged. The objectives outlined by the project team will then in turn be revised and reformulated by the teachers in the individual schools in relation to the peculiarities and idiosyncracies of their own teaching styles and contexts. Again we have already stressed the importance of this personal and professional autonomy of the teacher. Lastly, the pupils themselves will make their own revision, their own interpretations of what is being offered to them, and again we have suggested that it is right and proper that they should be able to do this. There will also be further modifications made by teachers in response to such pupil reaction. Thus any project team must plan in such a way as to allow for reinterpretation of its objectives at a number of levels as different agents in the educational process exercise their rights to decide on the form that process will take, although the team must also assume that its own efforts will in turn influence the kind of interpretation that others make (Blyth 1974).

It is thus at the level of short-term or even 'middle-ground' goals that the value problems and differences referred to earlier are most likely to arise, as different decisions are reached and different interpretations are made as to the most effective and appropriate means of satisfying these broad procedural principles. However, it is surely right that these differences of interpretation should be accepted and even encouraged, since, as we have seen, the greatest dangers derive from seeing the process of interpreting broad principles in terms of immediate decisions as a tightly deductive one. What is crucial, however, is that all of the interpretations that are made should individually and collectively reflect the original broad principles they are intended to implement (Hogben 1972).

Summary and conclusions

We have in this chapter attempted to examine critically some features of the trend which has been a feature of recent thinking about the curriculum towards focusing on the prespecification of objectives. We have unearthed several major difficulties of both a practical and a theoretical kind and have discovered that these difficulties are inherent not only in the particular schemes and taxonomies of educational objectives we have been offered but in the whole concept of this kind of approach to curriculum planning.

We then went on to suggest that the only solution to this dilemma is to adopt a much looser approach to the specification of objectives, regarding them as provisional and open to constant modification and reformulation, accepting the value and importance of long-term aims and recognizing these as statements of processes or principles rather than of extrinsic goals. We suggested too that these in a strange way might be easier to handle than shorter-term goals. We also stressed the importance of always being prepared to accept and welcome the unexpected. We noted that this accords much more with the practice of both teachers and other curriculum planners. Again, the worst difficulties arise when theoreticians polarize the issue and present us with an extreme model that is seldom if ever seen in practice. In fact, it may be that to a large extent the problem is a semantic one, that the confusions that clearly do exist in people's minds and in their practice in this area of curriculum planning arise at least to some extent from the use of words like 'objective' which bring with them connotations of extrinsic goals and introduce an imagery of the wrong kind into our discussions. As we have seen, when most people frame their objectives, these on close examination do look more like procedural principles than extrinsic goals or targets — certainly the treatment and use of them by teachers and others leads one to this interpretation — so that it may be that this is one area where our educational practice is better than our educational theory.

CHAPTER 3

CURRICULUM CONTENT

Many factors enter into decisions that are made about curriculum content, as we saw in Chapter 1, not least those factors that derive from the social pressures which are exerted on curriculum planners and demands that the schools should at least to some extent or for part of their curriculum seek to meet what appear to be the needs of the society they serve. However, we must also recognize that many fundamental decisions about the content of the curriculum have been made and continue to be made in the light of views that are held about the nature of knowledge. The history of education in the western world, from at least as far back as ancient Greece, reveals, for example, a concern to distinguish those areas of learning promoted by teachers in order to attain certain social goals from those aspects of learning that have seemed to have some independent and intrinsic right to inclusion in the curriculum and which, therefore, not only do not seek but positively eschew justification in instrumental terms. This was the point of the attraction felt and expressed in the ancient world for the idea of a liberal education, of the later concern with the education of the cultured gentleman and the resultant contrasting of liberal and vocational forms of education, a conflict which can still be discerned in the practice of the present day and which has led to some very clear and overt hierarchical distinctions between certain kinds of school subject. The same kind of thinking also expresses itself in modern theory through the differences that are now stressed between education as such, a term which it is suggested should and can only be appropriately applied to those activities that can be viewed and justified as intrinsically worthwhile, and other processes that also involve teaching and that schools also concern themselves with, such as socialization, training, instruction and the like (Peters 1965, 1966; Hirst and Peters 1970).

On the whole, such dispute as there has been over the inclusion of vocational or utilitarian learning in the curriculum has centred on the issue of whether this is an appropriate concern of schools at all or whether it should be their concern only in relation to the needs of those pupils who cannot cope with the intellectual demands of those subjects that have been felt to be intrinsically valuable (Bantock 1968, 1971). No one has felt it necessary to challenge their justification beyond that point, since if one accepts the ends to which they are instrumental it must follow that, other things being equal, one accepts the means to those ends.

There has been much disagreement, however, over the question of what is to be included in the curriculum for its own sake. Indeed, this question has been the focal point of educational debate since such debate began. It continues to be a highly controversial issue, since it is by no means a straightforward matter to identify those areas of knowledge that have value in their own right or that are to be seen as intrinsically worthwhile nor, indeed, even to demonstrate that there are areas of knowledge of which this is true.

This fundamental problem reveals itself today in a number of issues that loom large in current debate about education, questions such as those about the extent to which the content of the curriculum should be chosen in relation to the needs of society or the needs and interests of the pupils, questions about the nature of knowledge itself and whether there are considerations there that may resolve this issue for us, questions concerning the merits and defects, the possibility or impossibility of curriculum integration, not to mention the fundamental issue, to which we referred in Chapter 1, of finding any acceptable framework of values for curriculum planning. These are all current examples of this continuing debate and all of them are issues to which we must devote some detailed attention.

Culture and the curriculum

First, then, let us consider the case for basing decisions about the content of the curriculum on an analysis of the nature of society.

It must be recognized that schools exist in advanced or sophisticated societies as agencies for the handing on of the culture of the society, so that at least in part their purposes must be seen in terms of socialization or acculturation, attending to that induction of children into the ways of life of society which is achieved in more primitive societies by less formal methods. On this basis it has been argued that a good deal of what is to be taught in schools can be decided by reference to the culture of the society they are created to serve. This has been one of the root justifications of those who take a hard line on the question of curriculum content, since it has been argued that a major task of the school is to hand on to the next generation the 'common cultural heritage' of the society (Lawton 1975).

Even if one accepts the force of this claim in principle, in practice it creates more difficulties that it resolves. To begin with, difficulties arise because the term 'culture' has several different meanings. In particular, confusions are created by the fact that the term is used, by anthropologists for example, to denote in a purely descriptive sense all aspects of the ways of life of a particular society, as when we speak of the cultural patterns of a primitive community, while, on the other hand, it is also used to denote what is regarded as being best in the art and literature of any particular society. Thus a 'cultured gentleman' is not one who knows his way about the ways of life, the habits and beliefs of his society; he is a man who has been brought to appreciate those works of his fellows that are regarded as being among the finer achievements of the culture. When people talk then of basing the curriculum on the culture of the society, some of them are suggesting that we socialize the young, while others are encouraging us to frame the curriculum in terms of what is regarded as being best or most valuable among the intellectual and artistic achievements of the society. A leaning towards the latter interpretation, even when the problems of definition are recognized and a clear definition is offered, is likely to lead to a view of two or more cultures, a high and a low, or an upper class and a folk culture (Eliot 1948; Bantock 1968, 1971) and this has serious implications for curriculum planning and the practice of education generally which we must later examine. In particular, problems of both a theoretical and a practical kind arise when the distinction becomes associated with social class differences.

A second problem arises from the difficulty of establishing what is or should be the relationship between schools and the society in which they function. We have spoken so far as if the function of the schools is to transmit the culture of society, but there are those who would wish to argue that they exist rather to transform that culture, to act as positive agents of change. Do schools change society or do they themselves change in response to prior changes in society? These are nice questions. Even nicer are the issues we raise if we ask whether schools ought to be attempting to change society or merely to adjust to social changes. In reality, and perhaps in ideal terms too, it may be sufficient to recognize that both are interlinked and subject to many of the same influences and constraints so that changes occur in both *pari passu*, and this perhaps is how things should be.

Whatever view one takes of this issue, a further difficulty arises for those who wish to base decisions about the content of the curriculum on considerations of the culture of the society when we attempt to state in specific terms what that culture is. For it is clear that in a modern advanced industrial society no one pattern of life that can be called the culture of that society can be identified. Most modern societies are pluralist in nature; that is, it is possible to discern in them many different, and sometimes incompatible, cultures or sub-cultures. It does not follow that we must regard such sub-cultures as hierarchically related to each other but it is necessary to recognize them as being different from each other and it is also important to appreciate that most individual members of a society will participate in more than one of these sub-cultures at different times or in different aspects of their lives. Thus not only do most modern societies contain different ethnic groups, each with its own traditions, habits, beliefs, customs and so on, but they also contain different religious groups, different social groups, artistic groups, groups held together by many different shared interests, each of which will have its own norms, its own 'culture'.

The question as to whether schools should endeavour to promote a common culture or help divers groups to develop their own different cultures is a vexed one, not least in relation to those minority ethnic groups that are to be found in most societies. What concerns us more directly here, however, is the implication that even if we believe that the content of the curriculum should be based on the culture of the society, it will be impossible to assert with any real expectation of general acceptance what that culture is and therefore what the content of the curriculum should be. All that this line of argument will achieve is to bring us face to face with age-old issues concerning the appropriate educational provision for different social and ethnic groups, as we shall see when we come to consider in Chapter 7 the question of the common compulsory curriculum.

The problem is aggravated too by the fact that most societies are far from static entities and this implies that one feature of their culture is that it is changing, evolving, developing. Furthermore, western cultures 'are characterized not only by rapid change but also by deliberate change' (Taba 1962, p. 54). Technological change must also lead to changes in the norms, the values, the beliefs, the customs of a society; in other words, it must lead to a fluid culture. Moral change too is more difficult in many ways to handle. It is slower to take effect, since people shed or change their values more slowly and more reluctantly than they exchange their cars or their washing machines. Thus there is a time-lag between the technological changes and those that follow in the norms, customs and social institutions of the society (Taba 1962). Furthermore, moral change always requires much more careful and deliberate thought.

There are several aspects of this that have serious implications for education and the curriculum. Firstly, it makes even more impossible the task of deciding which aspects of the culture schools should initiate their pupils into. Secondly, it raises again the question of what the role of the school is or should be in relation to the culture of society, in particular whether it is there to transmit that culture or to transform it. Thirdly, it raises questions about what schools should be attempting to do for their pupils in a society that is subject to rapid change.

A recognition of the rapidity of social change and of the need for people to be equipped to cope with it and even to exercise some degree of control over it suggests that schools should in any case go beyond the notion of initiation of pupils into the culture of the society, beyond socialization and acculturation, to the idea of preparing pupils for the fact of social change itself, to adapt to and to initiate changes in the norms and values of the community. This requires that pupils be offered much more than a selection of the culture of the society as it exists at the time when they happen to be in schools, even if this could be identified and defined clearly enough for adequate educational practice.

Furthermore, if we are right to suggest that this is the only viable role the school can take in a rapidly changing society, if it can only equip pupils to take their place in such a society by developing in them the ability to think for themselves and make their own choices, then the question of whether the school is there to transmit or to transform the culture of society has already in part been answered. For the adoption of this kind of role takes the school well beyond the mere transmission of knowledge — a role that in a changing society would seem to be in any case untenable. If the school is not itself to transform the culture, it is certainly there to produce people who can and will transform it.

This is one source of a further problem that arises if we attempt to establish as the content of our curriculum those things which we regard as being the essential valuable elements of the culture. Recent practice has revealed very clearly that this can lead to the imposition on some pupils of a curriculum that is alien to them, which lacks relevance to their lives and to their experience outside the school and can ultimately bring about their alienation from and rejection of the education they are offered. This is probably the root cause of most of the problems that the educational system is facing today and it is certainly a real hazard if not an inevitable result of this kind of approach to curriculum planning.

These last points lead us on to a much more general weakness of this line of argument. For it will be apparent that even if we see it as the task of our schools to initiate pupils into the culture of the society, it will not be possible to offer them the whole of that culture, however it is defined. A selection will have to be made and, since this is so, any notion of the culture of the society, no matter how acceptable in definition or content, will in itself not provide us with appropriate criteria of selection. We will need to look elsewhere for justification of the selection we do make so that the arguments for a curriculum content based on the culture or cultures of society will not in itself take us very far towards finding a solution to our problem.

This bring us lastly to the realization that attempts to base decisions about the content of the curriculum on a consideration of the nature of society are, if interpreted in this way, essentially utilitarian arguments; they seek a social or sociological justification for curriculum content and therefore imply that that justification is to be sought outside the activity or the knowledge or the content itself, a procedure which we have already suggested is incompatible with the notion of education as such.

This charge can only be avoided if they go further and argue that what is valuable in the culture is valuable not merely because it is part of the culture but because it has some intrinsic merit which justifies its place not only on the curriculum but also in society itself. Thus some curriculum theorists, such as Paul Hirst, argue for the inclusion of certain areas of knowledge in the curriculum on the grounds that these are those forms of knowledge that constitute rationality itself, that they represent what it means to be rational, so that without them nothing that can be called 'education' is possible since education is seen as essentially concerned to develop the rational mind (Hirst 1965, 1969; Hirst and Peters 1970).

If this is what is being claimed, it is of course a completely different argument from that which seeks justification in the culture itself and it does bring us up against the whole issue of the nature of knowledge and whether any body of knowledge has or can have an intrinsic, objective, absolute value or status. The focus of the question, therefore, continues to be the nature of knowledge and any attempt to seek for a justification of curriculum content in terms that are not instrumental or utilitarian must start with an examination of what knowledge is.

Knowledge and the curriculum

The question 'what is knowledge?' can be interpreted in several ways. It can be taken as a psychological question about how people come to have knowledge, about the psychological and behavioural changes that occur when learning takes place. It can equally be interpreted as a philosophical, semantic question about what it means to know something, what kind of behavioural changes are to count as evidence of the acquisition of knowledge, rather than of, say, the development of habits or fixed responses to certain stimuli. It is in this sense that it is often argued that the term 'knowledge' can only properly be used of that kind of learning that involves understanding, that knowledge *that* something is the case must always be accompanied by knowledge *why* it is the case, since only if we insist on this can we distinguish knowledge from belief, opinion or mere guesswork.

It is this latter point that leads us on to the question that is central to our discussion of curriculum content. Once again we must note the inter-relatedness of these questions, but the questions that are most relevant to our immediate concerns are not those about the knower but those about the nature of knowledge itself and, in particular, questions about what will constitute grounds for the claim that we know something to be the case rather than merely believe or guess it to be so. In other words, what is it by virtue of which we are justified in claiming knowledge? What are the criteria by which we can assess the validity of knowledge? Interpreted in this way, the question 'what is knowledge?' becomes almost synonymous with the question 'what is truth?' and its central relevance to decisions of curriculum content will be clear, since it will be impossible to justify the inclusion of certain areas of knowledge in the curriculum for their own sake unless evidence can be produced as to their truth content, objectivity or intrinsic value.

This question has been a major concern of philosophers since the time of Plato. Indeed, it could be argued that this is the focal point of philosophy itself since all branches of philosophy — ethics, aesthetics, politics and so on — can be seen as centrally engaged in a search for what will constitute knowledge in each particular field. Inevitably a number of different theories about the nature and structure of knowledge have been offered, all or most of which are still in vogue and it would be for many reasons desirable that we should consider these in great detail, firstly, because particular theories about the nature of knowledge are implicit in or assumed by all theories that are proposed as bases for curriculum development and planning and, secondly and more importantly, because the assumptions about the nature of knowledge that such theories make are often left unquestioned and accepted uncritically. In other words, the epistemological bases of the curriculum are too little understood by curriculum theorists and most theories about the curriculum need to be looked at very critically and rigorously from this point of view.

However, we must content ourselves here with a brief survey of the main issues, a procedure that may be more acceptable since it begins to appear to me that the most important point for curriculum theorists to understand is perhaps not the details of particular epistemological theories, although clearly they should grasp them if they intend to base their own theories on them, but rather the variety of theories that have been offered and the fact that each of them is inevitably tentative and hypothetical and fails to offer an account of knowledge that is generally acceptable.

Two main kinds of theory have emerged during the development of Western European philosophy, those rationalist views that take as their starting point the supremacy of the intellect over other human faculties and stress that true knowledge is that which is achieved by the mind in some way independently of the information provided by the senses, and those empiricist views which have taken a contrary stance and maintained that knowledge of the world about us can only be derived from the evidence that the world offers us through the use of our senses.

This dispute reflects a distinction that has characterized Western European philosophy from the beginning between the idea of the fallibility of the senses as sources of information and views that some have held of the infallibility of the intellect. Thus such philosophers as Plato, Descartes and Kant have offered various versions of a rationalist epistemology which have shared the basic conviction that the evidence of our senses is misleading but that the rational mind can attain true knowledge independently of the senses by apprehending what lies beyond those sense impressions or in some way introducing a rational structure to our understanding of them.

Such theories, seeing knowledge as essentially independent of the observations of our senses, inevitably lead to a view of knowledge as in some sense God-given, 'out-there' and independent of the knower, having a status that is untouched by and owes nothing to the human condition of the beings who possess the knowledge they are concerned with. Thus for Plato, and especially for Aristotle, the act of contemplation of the supreme forms of human knowledge is a godlike act, through which man transcends his human condition and achieves, albeit momentarily, the supreme bliss of the life of pure intellect perpetually enjoyed by God. For Kant too, at a more mundane level, the task of establishing a critique of knowledge is essentially one of discovering those elements of knowledge which owe nothing to our nature as human beings, those which are derived from pure reason and have nothing to do with human feelings or passions.

The other main kind of epistemological theory, empiricism, can be seen as a reaction to the mysticism of these rationalist views. Its fundamental tenet is well expressed in the claim of John Locke, the founder of the empiricist movement, that no knowledge comes into the mind except through the gates of the senses. The mind of the new-born child is seen as a *tabula rasa*, a clean sheet, 'void of all characters, without any ideas'. Such knowledge as it acquires, it acquires through sensation and reflection, that is, by what its senses tell it and by its own reflective introspection and interpretation of its perceptions.

A basic position such as this leads inevitably to a less confident view of knowledge and to a greater awareness of the tentative nature of human knowledge, since it is agreed by everyone that the rationalists are right in claiming that the evidence of our senses is unreliable. Indeed, one of the earliest and most ardent exponents of the empiricist view of knowledge, David Hume, came to the conclusion that no knowledge was possible at all or, at least, that we could have little certainty in our knowledge of the world about us. 'If we believe that fire warms or water refreshes, 'tis only because it costs us too much pains to think otherwise.' It is not perhaps necessary to go as far to the other extreme as this, but it is necessary, if one takes such a view, to recognize at the very least the hypothetical nature of knowledge, as present day empiricist theories do (Ayer 1936, 1946).

Thus a number of recent theories of knowledge and theories of education have begun from the conviction that human knowledge has to be treated in a far more tentative way than many who take a rationalist view would concede and that, in relation to curriculum planning, we are in no position to be dogmatic about its content. The whole pragmatist movement, as promoted by John Dewey, which has been highly influential in the recent development of educational practice, has been founded on a view of knowledge as hypothetical and therefore subject to constant change, modification and evolution. Such a view requires us to be hesitant about asserting the value of any body of knowledge or its right to inclusion in the curriculum and encourages us to accept that knowledge is to be equated rather with experience, so that what it means for a child to acquire knowledge is that he should have experieneces which he can himself use as the basis for the framing of hypotheses to explain and gain control over the environment in which he lives. In other words, we cannot impose what is knowledge for us upon him; we must assist him to develop his own knowledge, his own hypotheses, which will be different from ours if the process of evolution is to go on.

This certainly results in a view of education as a much more personal activity than any rationalist could acknowledge. It may also suggest that knowledge itself is personal and subjective. This, however, is not a view that Dewey himself subscribed to. He believed that the proper model for all knowledge is that of scientific knowledge, where hypotheses are framed and modified according to publicly agreed criteria, so that while such knowledge has no permanent status it is objective in so far as it at least enjoys current acceptance by everyone.

Others have gone much further than this, however, and have suggested that knowledge cannot be seen as having even a current universal acceptance. This is the main thrust of the recent dramatic developments in sociology towards the generation of a sociology of knowledge. For it has been argued here not only that knowledge is a human product but that it is the product of particular social groups, 'a product of the informal understandings negotiated among members of an organized intellectual collectivity' (Blum 1971). On this view, then, knowledge is socially constructed and, since socially constructed knowledge is ideology, any attempt to make decisions about the content of the curriculum that are based on some views of what kinds of knowledge are valuable has to be seen as an attempt to impose one particular ideology on children and thus to achieve some kind of social control over them either deliberately or merely as a by-product of one's practice. Debate about the content of the curriculum is thus seen as dispute between conflicting ideologies.

Others have gone even further than this and stressed the phenomenological or existentialist claim that all knowledge is personal and subjective, that every individual's knowledge is the result of his own completely unique perceptions of his own world. As a result of arguments of this kind, we have demands from people like Illich, Freire and others that society should be de-schooled and the process of education made less formal, and from others that we should merely consider again the content of the curriculum and endeavour to base it on the 'common sense knowledge' of the pupil rather than the 'educational knowledge' of the teacher (Keddie 1971). In this way it is suggested we will avoid the alienation we referred to earlier which, it is claimed, is experienced by children who see no point or meaning in the content of what is presented to them and we will also repudiate the charge that we are endeavouring to gain control of them by indoctrinating them with the values, the ideology, of one dominant section of the community.

We have thus come full circle, since we are back with the problem of conflicting sub-cultures and we seem to have drawn a blank in our attempts to find a solution to our problem. For we were attempting to discover some criteria within the nature of knowledge itself which would enable us to choose between conflicting cultures or to make a selection from what seemed to be the common culture and this we have failed to do. There is no universally accepted theory of knowledge and the theories that appear to have the strongest claims on our acceptance are those that tell us that they cannot establish the kind of objective status for knowledge that we require in order to make decisions about the content of the curriculum entirely on the basis of this kind of consideration.

In fact, our brief survey of some of the major features of what philosophers and others have said about knowledge has suggested that epistemological considerations in themselves can provide no positive help to curriculum planners, since one can find no clear, hard and fast theory of knowledge upon which any firm choice of curriculum content can be based. Similarly, as we shall see later, they offer no clear-cut basis for the development of an objective framework of values within which such decisions can be made.

This also highlights a fundamental tension, or even a contradiction, in Denis Lawton's model of curriculum planning which we considered briefly in Chapter 1. We saw there that he is suggesting that in making decisions about the curriculum we look to both philosophical assertions about the nature of knowledge and to sociological considerations about such things as social and technological change and that we balance these against each other. It should now be apparent, however, that if those philosophical assertions are such as to promote a view of knowledge as having a 'God-given' status, then they must also require of us that we do not, or even cannot, modify or compromise this God-given status by reference to mundane sociological considerations of the here-and-now of particular societies. If, on the other hand, these philosophical considerations do not lead to this view of knowledge, then they must lead to a view of it as socially constructed in some way, so that they are not fundamentally different kinds of consideration from the sociological considerations themselves.

Again, therefore, either epistemological considerations of a purely philosophical kind must dominate curriculum planning, no matter how socially irrelevant the curriculum is that they lead to, or it must be accepted that they are of no real help in curriculum planning at all.

If epistemology is of any value to the curriculum planner, that value derives only from the fact that this kind of enquiry can illuminate and introduce some clarity into our discussions of the curriculum, since such excursions into the theory of knowledge do help to point up some of the difficulties that curriculum planners face in this area and to bring out the assumptions implicit in some theories about the curriculum. They also provide some negative evidence as to where solutions to these problems are not to be found and suggest, therefore, both that we look elsewhere for solutions and that there are real dangers in expecting these solutions ever to be so conclusive that we can be dogmatic about them. For they also reveal that some of the difficulties that we meet in curriculum planning are a direct result of the adoption of one particular theory of knowledge on the assumption that it can not only help to solve our problems but that it can in itself provide a final answer to them. In other words, too close an adherence to any one theory of what knowledge is or of what is knowledge is likely in itself to generate problems, some of which, such as the problems of curriculum integration that we shall consider in Chapter 4, might not otherwise have existed.

If no justification is to be found in epistemology, then, and if at the same time an appeal to the nature of society reveals as bewildering a variety of demands as we have suggested, there remain only two possibilities. Either we must look elsewhere for a basis for our choice of curriculum content, to the nature of the child, for example, to his needs or his interests, or we must find some basis for a framework of values which will enable us to make a choice among bodies of knowledge or among the cultures and sub-cultures of society. If we do the former, there is a distinct possibility that we will come up with not one curriculum but many — as many perhaps as there are pupils — and this will in turn raise difficulties of its own. We must now consider, therefore, firstly, the suggestion that a consideration of the many aspects of child nature be used as the criterion of choice, and, secondly, the problem of establishing a framework of values within which choice of curriculum content may be made.

Child-centred education

The idea that in seeking answers to our questions about what should be taught we look to an examination of the nature of the child is not new; it is certainly not a product of the twentieth century. The revolt against the traditional view of education as concerned with the purveying of certain kinds of abstract knowledge and the development of rationality was begun by Rousseau in the eighteenth century and carried forward by other, perhaps more influential, educators, such as Froebel and Montessori in the last century. The main thrust of that revolt was against the idea that we plan our educational practices by a consideration of knowledge and that we begin to look instead to the children who are the objects of those practices and plan according to what we can discover about them. It is for this reason that this general movement has been termed 'child-centred'.

What is recent is the rigorous examination of what this entails, since for many years, while admittedly encouraging a more humane approach to education and requiring a more careful consideration of the child's feelings and his reactions to educational practices, it was highly suspect theoretically, leading more to the generation of a romantic reverence for childhood and of 'beautiful thoughts' about children than to any rigorous analysis of what education fundamentally is or should be. It is one thing to claim that education should be planned according to what we know about the nature of children; it is quite another to spell out precisely how our knowledge of children should be reflected in our educational planning. Thus some of the early theories seemed to suggest that no planning should be done at all, since they advised us to leave the child alone to develop naturally, to grow like a plant in a garden, free from the corrupting or confining influences of adults.

With theories such as these it is very difficult to decide what practical provisions they should lead to. They may be helpful in our attempts to decide on appropriate methods but they offer no criteria by which we can make choices of suitable content. It is largely because of this ambivalence that attempts have been made in more recent times to produce more coherent accounts of the practical implications of this fundamental view of the central role of child nature in curriculum planning.

Three related kinds of answer have been offered to this question — claims that our main concern should be the needs of the child, attempts to give a coherent account of the nature of growth and assertions that the content of the curriculum should be decided by reference to the interests of the children. We must look at each of these briefly in an attempt to assess whether they will offer us the yardstick we are looking for.

Needs

The idea that we should begin our curriculum planning by attempting to discover what children need is an attractive one that appears at first sight to dovetail naturally into a theory of education that takes as its main focus the nature of children and suggests that that should be our first concern in planning educational provision. The whole thrust of the naturalist 'child-centred' movement, as we have seen, is away from the view that education should be planned by reference to the nature of knowledge or the needs of society towards claiming that the main, perhaps the sole, concern should be with the nature of the child and, therefore, with his needs. This whole movement gave great impetus to the development of the study of child psychology, since clearly if we are to pay heed to the nature of children we need to discover as much as we can about that nature and the translation of this into the idea of needs was one attempt by educational psychologists to spell out what kind of educational provision this concern with child nature should lead to. In fact, the concept of need has been an important one in psychology generally and was therefore a popular and attractive notion to educationists when education theory was dominated by the results of psychological researches.

Like all of these theories, the idea of needs does lead to important changes in our methods and approaches in education but it is not one that will help us with decisions of content, since it is not a concept that will hold up to any depth of analysis (Dearden 1968; Wilson 1971).

In the first place, the argument that we can resolve questions of what anyone ought to have by reference to what they are seen to need involves an illicit process from 'is' to 'ought' which can never constitute sound reasoning and which, amongst other things, begs a good many questions of a moral and social kind. For it may be claimed that the whole fabric of society is held together by the ability of most people to go without some of the things they might feel they need in the interests of social cohesion.

Furthermore, even if this were not so, the problem of identifying needs still remains. It may well be that much human behaviour, and especially the motivation for that behaviour, is explicable in terms of the reduction of needs through their satisfaction or part satisfaction (Maslow 1954), since clearly if a felt need is reduced in some way the pattern of behaviour associated with that reduction will be reinforced. But to characterize all learning as being of this type is to go too far and in any case, even if this were the model for all learning, we would still be left with the problem of evaluating between needs, of deciding which patterns of behaviour should be reinforced by these processes of need reduction, since the notion of need in itself, as we have just seen, does not provide us with the criteria of evaluation, with a framework of values, with grounds for asserting what ought to be done.

This becomes apparent when we consider the detailed accounts of human needs that the psychologists offer us. Maslow, for example, identified three kinds of need — primary needs for food, air, sleep and so on, emotional needs for such things as love and security and social needs for acceptance by one's peers and such like (Maslow 1954). However, the further we move up this hierarchy of needs, the more problematic our acceptance of them becomes and even greater difficulties arise over questions of whether, and in particular how, these needs are to be satisfied. A moment's consideration will reveal this.

In short, the term 'need' does not offer us a straight objective description of certain features of human nature that we can use as a basis for planning any kind of social or educational provision. At all but the very basic levels it is impossible to distinguish what we need from what we want or, worse, what someone else thinks we ought to want or ought to have. We still have to choose between the things that people need or think they need and again the notion of need in itself will not provide us with the criterion by reference to which we can make such choices.

Growth

Much the same problem arises when we attempt to explicate the demand that we base our curriculum planning on a consideration of the nature of the child by reference to the idea of natural growth. For the idea of natural growth in itself is of little real help to educationists since what they really want to know is how, when and where they might be justified in interfering with that growth. Similarly, analogies drawn from gardening are not very helpful since the main need of the gardener is to know when to interfere with the natural development of his flowers, tomatoes or hops. The notion of growth in itself cannot enable us to distinguish education from maturation and, therefore, cannot provide us with any of the criteria we are looking for (Dearden 1968).

To speak of guided growth, as, for example, John Dewey does, is to do no more than push the question one stage backwards. For we now have to ask what criteria we should appeal to in deciding how to guide children's growth. Again we see that the idea of growth is helpful to us in reaching decisions about appropriate methods in education, since it suggests that these should be such as to ensure that the development of children involves fundamental and permanent changes and that their learning should not be superficial, that it should not consist of 'inert ideas' (Whitehead 1932) that remain as outward manifestations rather

than becoming inner transformations, but should involve understanding and knowledge in the full sense. Thus it has led to claims such
as that of the Hadow Report of 1931 that the curriculum should be
thought of in terms of activity and experience rather than knowledge to
be acquired and facts to be stored. We have noted already the central role
played by the notion of experience in Dewey's educational philosophy.
There is also support for this view of education in the work of people
such as Piaget and Bruner who view education as a process of cognitive
growth and see the main concerns of the teacher as being to assist pupils
to acquire those concepts which will enable them to interact
successfully with their environment.

Some choice must be made, however, of the particular concepts we are
to help children to acquire, so that again we see it is not sufficient even
to define growth in terms of conceptual development. Nor does the
notion of guided growth help us in decisions of content. The idea of
guidance in itself implies direction; a guided activity is an activity with
an end or aim in view. To stop a man in the street and ask him to guide
you without knowing where you want to go is to invite psychiatric help
or perhaps something more violent. However, neither the notion of
growth nor that of guidance can in themselves offer answers to this
question of direction.

Dewey's own answer to this problem is an interesting one. He is aware
that growth must be directed and he is also aware that this implies the
existence of some kind of goal. On the other hand, his view of
knowledge, as we have seen, will not allow him to produce any theory
that implies that teachers, parents, adults generally or even society as a
whole have the answers to this question of goals, since, as we have seen,
for him knowledge must be allowed to develop and evolve and this
cannot happen if the knowledge of one generation is imposed on the
next, no matter how gently this is done. His answer is to assert that the
only criterion we can use in attempting to evaluate one kind of activity,
one body of content, one set of experiences in relation to others is an
assessment of the extent to which each is likely to be productive of
continued experience and development. Thus he speaks of an
'experiential continuum' (Dewey 1938, Ch. 3) which is for him the
essence of education as a continuous lifelong process and which offers
us the principle by which we can reach decisions concerning the content
of each child's curriculum, that principle being always to choose that
activity or those experiences likely to be most productive of further
experience.

There is a good deal that is of value in this concept of the teacher as one who keeps constantly open the options available to each pupil and tries to ensure continuous development and progress, for ever widening horizons and steering pupils away from any experience that will have the effect of closing them down. The idea is an attractive one and as a principle to underlie all of our educational practice it would appear to be of great importance.

As a practical criterion by which we can pronounce upon the competing claims of different activities or bodies of knowledge for inclusion in a curriculum, however, it does not take us very far, as any teacher will know. Furthermore, it does not help us to decide where or how this continuous process is to start, what experiences we are to offer pupils initially to get them started or, perhaps more importantly, which experiences we should steer them away from. Nor is it enough to suggest that this kind of decision can be left to the evidence the psychologists offer us concerning ages and stages of development. Again this is not enough, because again it is merely the argument from needs in a slightly more sophisticated guise. We still require a framework of values to enable us to make choices among the many possibilities that exist for pupil activity both at the beginning of and throughout this process of education by means of continuous and productive experiences. There are many directions in which growth can be guided and many of these will be as productive and as praiseworthy as each other, just as there are many different ways in which I can train up the roses in my garden. We still need to be able to assess which of these directions is the most appropriate or likely to be the most prolific, and the idea of continuous experience offers little if anything more than the idea of continuous growth itself. It will not provide us with the practical answers we need.

Interests

It is partly for this reason that we have been offered a third device by which it is suggested we can implement at a practical level the idea that education should be based on the nature of the child — a recommendation that we should base our decisions concerning the content of the curriculum on a consideration of the interests of the child. Again this was a feature of John Dewey's philosophy of education and this theory has recently been developed more fully in an attempt to resolve some of the difficulties that a 'child-centred' approach to education presents (Wilson 1971). Briefly, it is suggested that we plan our curriculum not in the light of what we think to be the nature of knowledge nor by reference to what appear to be the requirements of the society or culture in which we live, but in response to what we can find that is actually of interest to the children themselves.

At one level such an approach has obvious advantages. For there is no doubt that children do work better and learn more effectively when they are interested in what they are being required to do. Conversely, it is a lack of interest in the work that teachers require of them that is responsible for the failure to learn and the ultimate alienation and disaffection of many pupils. Every good teacher appreciates this elementary fact of child psychology and all teachers endeavour to make their lessons and the work in which they are engaging their pupils interesting in as many ways as possible — by using all kinds of visual aids, for example, or by incorporating practical work and sometimes even organizing outside visits. We all know that children will learn more in one visit to a museum, provided that visit is properly organized, than in ten lessons offering them oral descriptions of what could be seen there. Again we note therefore that this kind of approach will lead to an improvement in our methodology; we will be better teachers for taking account of children's interests in planning how we will present our material to them.

Interpreted in this way, this approach to educational planning through a consideration of children's interests, therefore, is no more than a methodological device for improving our teaching of what we want them to learn, by making them interested in what we feel they should be interested in or by starting from their interests and leading them on to what we want them to do.

However, it has been argued (Wilson 1971) that this use of children's interests trivializes them by using them as means to the achievement of our ends rather than recognizing them as having for the child an intrinsic value. It is certainly the case that such an approach will not solve the problem we are concerned with here; it provides us with no criteria to decide what we should encourage children to be interested in or how we should develop the interests they already have. We have to look elsewhere for a basis upon which we can build our curriculum content, if we interpret the idea of using children's interests in this way.

However, there is a further and deeper level at which we have been offered this idea of children's interests as a basis for our curriculum planning. It has been suggested (Wilson 1971) that we should actually decide on the content of our curriculum by reference to the interests of children and that we should plan our work, not in order to use these interests to achieve our own purposes, but to help the children to pursue their interests more effectively and with more discrimination and to organize their experiences in such a way as to extend and deepen those interests and gain a clearer view of their intrinsic value.

If education is concerned with activities that have an intrinsic value rather than with those that are instrumental to the achievement of ends beyond themselves and if, as we have argued, it is not possible to identify certain activities as being characterized in some way as having this intrinsic merit, then we must accept that intrinsic value, like beauty, is to be found not inhering in objects or activities but in the eye of the valuer. that those activities that are intrinsically valuable are those that the children do actually value in themselves and that, as a result, a curriculum can only be truly described as educational if its content consists of those things that pupils are interested in.

In brief, then, it is argued that a consideration of the interests of children is central not only to an effective methodology but also to the educational content of our curriculum. It is further argued that only an approach such as this will enable us to avoid the problems that arise when a curriculum is planned by reference to other considerations and, as a result, lacks relevance, becomes reified and leads to the total alienation of pupils from their education.

What is being recommended here is very clear. If we are to avoid all the ills that it is said follow for many pupils when we as teachers decide for them what they shall learn and thus impose our values on them, we can only do this by letting them decide what the content of their education will be by revealing to us what they are interested in. Such an approach creates many practical problems for teachers and others in matters such as the organization of work in the classroom, the planning and setting of public examinations and so on. None of these, however, would be insuperable if we were convinced on theoretical grounds that this was the only proper approach to the planning of curriculum content. There are, however, several difficulties of a more theoretical kind with this view and we must consider some of these now.

In the first place, the identification of children's interests is not the straightforward matter it may appear to be at first glance (White 1964, 1967; Wilson 1971). Distinguishing an abiding interest from an inclination, a passing whim or a temporary fad, even at the conceptual level, is not easy and clearly we must first know what sorts of thing interests are if we are to use them as the basis of our curriculum planning.

But even if we sort that question out there still remain many difficulties in actually recognizing what we are looking for and identifying children's interests. It is clearly not enough to think only in terms of what children enjoy doing since pursuing an interest is not necessarily always a pleasurable activity, as I have often found as I have worked on this book. Some interests which people pursue with enormous devotion and enthusiasm are of a kind that appear to be characterized mainly by being 'nice when you stop'. Nor is it merely a matter of asking children what their interests are, since they cannot always tell us, and their behaviour can often be misleading, an appearance or show of interest not always being a reliable indication of the existence of a real interest in the full sense.

Secondly, we need to know more than we do about the origins of children's interests and we need to give some thought to this before too readily accepting them as the basis of their education. A child whose home background is a very limited one is unlikely to have a very wide range of interests and we may not be doing him the greatest of favours by underwriting those limitations. For all children there are likely to be areas of understanding they will miss if we only attend to what they are already interested in and, even though the dangers of reification and alienation will immediately again rear their heads, there will be occasions when teachers will need to stimulate interests in children where they do not already exist. If this is not so, then we run the risk of depriving some children of large areas of experience that they might otherwise have profited from — a problem we shall need to consider again when we look at the issues of the common curriculum. If, on the other hand, this is so, then again the presence or absence of an interest will not in itself constitute the central criterion for deciding whether a particular activity or body of knowledge should be included in our curriculum or not.

The same difficulty also arises when we consider the question of selection of interests. It is likely to be the case that some of children's interests will appear to be of a trivial kind, unless we define interest in such a way as to exclude all such. Certainly not all interests will appear to be equally valuable or important and some may even seem to require discouragement on moral or social grounds. In this context we are always given the example of the child whose interest lies in pulling wings off insects — I have never met this child myself, although I have often wanted to — and clearly in such cases the interest is not to be encouraged on the mere grounds that it is an interest. Furthermore, every child will have many interests and it will not be possible, even if it were desirable, for him to pursue them all, so that again choices need to be made among these interests and decisions taken as to which of them should be developed. Again, therefore, we need some criterion of choice other than the fact that certain interests are believed to exist. As we have seen already, to say that education should be child-centred, in whatever sense we use the term, cannot be to be advocating complete freedom of activity for the children and, if the teacher is to play any part at all in the child's education, he must select the activities that he will encourage and promote. He must also decide on the directions in which he will promote them since there are countless ways in which an interest can be developed and not all of them will appear equally valuable or desirable. We might appeal here to the idea of the experiential continuum that we have already considered. It may appear that our solution lies in suggesting that the interests of the child should be seen as the starting point for the continuous experience of which Dewey speaks and the choice of interests and decisions as to the direction in which they are to be developed made in the light of the single criterion of how continuously productive and fertile they appear to be. However, as we saw when we considered the idea of the experiential continuum itself, it does not provide us with the criterion by which we can make the choices it creates for us. Nor does the notion of interests take us very much further. This idea in itself, therefore, will not provide us with the criterion we are looking for to decide on the content of our curriculum. We still need something else to appeal to in reaching real practical decisions.

As we have seen throughout this discussion, this is the difficulty with all so-called 'child-centred' theories. All attempts to base decisions concerning the content of the curriculum on a consideration of the nature of children are seen on closer analysis to offer us useful advice on our methods, our approaches to teaching, our attitudes to children; they offer us no more satisfactory solutions to the questions facing us, no more adequate a framework of values for choices of content than considerations derived from the nature of knowledge or the needs and nature of society.

We must finally turn, therefore, to a consideration of whether it is possible to find any framework of values within which a choice of curriculum content can be made, whether it is possible to establish any criteria by which different kinds of knowledge can be evaluated against each other or upon which claims can be based for the inclusion of some rather than others in the curriculum.

Values and the curriculum

It is only relatively recently that doubts have been expressed about the validity of the claim that certain kinds of knowledge are inherently more valuable or more important than others. For Plato there was no doubt that there was a very clear hierarchy of knowledge with philosophy at its peak and this, along with so many of the fundamental assumptions of Platonism, went unquestioned up to the time when the empiricists offered the challenge of a completely new approach to the question of knowledge. The fundamental principle of that hierarchy was that the greater the level of abstraction the more status a particular kind of knowledge had. Thus, in addition to the claims we examined earlier for the superiority of intellectual knowledge over sense-experience of the phenomena of the physical world, Plato also asserts that gradations must be recognized within the realms of intellectual knowledge according to degrees of abstraction, with philosophy, or dialectic as he calls it at this point in his argument, as a form of knowledge that he sees as totally abstract and not hypothetical in any way, at the pinnacle or as the coping stone (Plato, *Republic* § 134).

The influence of that kind of thinking on curriculum development, or non-development, over the years should not need to be spelled out to anyone who has spent any time teaching in our schools or colleges or universities. It is also worth noting here that another of the arguments Plato uses to support his claim for the superiority of philosophy over all other forms of knowledge is that all philosophers believe this to be so and they are the only people who are in a position to know. Furthermore, in his ideal society all other citizens will have been brought up to accept this and to obey the philosopher-kings without question. In other words, this is a view which, as we suggested earlier, leads to the generation of two or three levels of culture, two or three kinds of curriculum, and two or three classes of people within society.

We have already noted that an empiricist view of knowledge destroys this reified 'out-there' status of knowledge and, once that has gone, there is no basis for any such hierarchy. It was as a result of the empiricist movement, therefore, that the existence of qualitative differences between knowledge and types of human activity came first to be challenged. The full implications of this became clear in the doctrine of Utilitarianism as developed by Jeremy Bentham.

Bentham's main concern was to establish a moral principle for legislation and he found that principle in the notion of social utility — the greatest good of the greatest number. Thus, in his *Theory of Legislation*, he tells us, 'the end and aim of a legislator should be the HAPPINESS of the people. In matters of legislation, GENERAL UTILITY should be his guiding principle,' and again, 'The *Principle of Utility*, accordingly, consists in taking as our starting point, in every process of ordered reasoning, the calculus of comparative estimate of pains and pleasures, and in not allowing any other idea to intervene.'

Such a comparative estimate of pleasures and pains, however, results in the greatest good being conceived in terms entirely of social utility and not by reference to some metaphysical notion of quality. The only kinds of difference that he will allow between pleasures and between pains are quantitative differences, those to be found in their degrees of purity, intensity, duration and so on; he does not see any basis upon which we can make qualitative distinctions by claiming that certain pleasures are 'better' or 'more worthwhile' than others or upon which we can distinguish between good and bad taste. Thus John Stuart Mill in his essay on Bentham quotes him as saying, 'quantity of pleasure being equal, push-pin is as good as poetry'.

The implications of this view for education are clearly serious and it was as much because of his concern to promote education as for any other reason that John Stuart Mill endeavoured to reframe the whole doctrine in such a way as to introduce or re-introduce the notion of qualitative differences between kinds of pleasure and kinds of human activity (West 1965). There is of course a fundamental tension between Utilitarianism itself, which takes at root an instrumental view of value, and the notion of intrinsic value, so that inevitably this resulted in its becoming a totally different doctrine as a result of Mill's work. Nevertheless, this is the point of Mill's often-quoted assertion that 'It is better to be a human being dissatisfied than a pig satisfied; better to be a Socrates dissatisfied than a fool satisfied' (J. S. Mill, *Utilitarianism*, Ch. II). However, the argument he produces to support this claim is remarkably weak for a case that is so crucial and also very reminiscent of Plato's argument for the superiority of philosophy. For he goes on to say, 'And if the fool, or the pig, are of a different opinion, it is because they only know their own side of the question. The other party to the comparison knows both sides' (ibid.).

This particular battle still rages, especially in relation to the curriculum (Wilson 1967; Peters 1967), and clearly it is of crucial importance. It has resulted in a questioning of the content of education of a kind which at one time would have been unthinkable. For as long as the view of values as fixed and unchangeable held sway, the model of education that it gave rise to remained virtually unquestioned. That model is the Platonic model of the slow ascent of the individual up the ladder of knowledge towards greater degrees of abstraction or, to use his own metaphor, the gradual emergence from the dark cave of ignorance into the light of the sun and finally to the contemplation of the sun itself. This is a view that can still be detected today as much in the un-questioned assumptions of some people's thinking about education as in certain explicit statements about it. Even the metaphors are similar, the child being seen as the barbarian at the gates and education as the process of gradual admission to the citadel of civilization (Peters 1965). The arguments too have a familiar ring to them since the superiority of certain kinds of human activity is still argued in terms of such things as cognitive content, seriousness and intrinsic value (Peters 1966). The means/end aspect of the Platonic model has been rightly criticized and rejected but all else remains fundamentally much the same.

However, the difficulties have been revealed of establishing the claim that any kind of activity has an intrinsic value over and above the value that individual human beings place on it or that value in some way inheres in certain kinds of activity. Values are not entities that have some kind of existence of their own even in some metaphysical sense. Valuing is an activity; it is something people do. Only confusion can result when we allow such activities to become reified because the vagaries of English grammar allow certain verbal functions to be performed by the use of nouns. This is a fallacy common to a number of philosophical problems. Valuing can only be an activity and, as is the case with all activities, different people do it differently.

Furthermore, such a view of values as objective is based on a view of knowledge as 'out-there' and God-given, a view that we saw earlier is at the very least highly questionable. If knowledge is not seen as having this sort of objective status independent of the knower, it is difficult to know what basis there could be for claiming that some activities have an intrinsic value independent of the value placed on them by individual human beings, and even more difficult to establish what these activities are.

Several further points must be made which derive from this basic feature of values.

In the first place, it is perhaps worth taking up again a point we made in Chapter 2 when discussing behavioural objectives. For a view of values as deriving their validity from the actual choices made by individuals is another essential feature of a view of man as an active rather than as a passive being, a creature whose behaviour is the result of his own choices and purposes and not merely of the causal effects of external events. Such a view of values, therefore, follows naturally from the idea of the autonomy of the individual and must lead to the rejection of any study of education or planning of the curriculum that is based on a behaviourist model of man.

It is worth going further too and stressing again that it is this which makes it possible to distinguish education from other activities such as training or conditioning. We have several times had cause to refer to the development of autonomy as an essential feature of any distinctive concept of education (Peters 1965, 1966). We are here faced with one of the implications of that. Such a concept of education must acknowledge that autonomy for the individual implies his right to do his own valuing and not merely to be brought to recognize certain values for which, in Platonic style, objective status is claimed.

On the other hand, the need to make choices in the absence of any criteria of choice presents us with the archetypal dilemma of the existentialist and is conducive to nothing so much as the nausea that Jean Paul Sartre and others speak of. We must not, however, assume that it implies that we must accept all knowledge as being of equal value. To say that qualitative differences between kinds of knowledge and kinds of human activity cannot be argued for is not to say that we must accept them all as being of equal merit. Of course, we will all make distinctions of this kind.

Nor does making choices become a matter of just 'plumping' for this or that, sticking a pin into a list or tossing a coin. A good many choices will be made by reference to factors of an empirical kind, since many will involve a selection of means rather than ends. There is clearly difficulty, however, in arguing for ultimate values or even stating to one's own satisfaction the grounds upon which one adheres to them. It is the justification of these ultimate values which, as we have seen, must always be offered at a subjective level.

This raises, of course, the thorny question of who is to make the choices, who is to decide on the content of the curriculum. Shall it be left to the pupils themselves, the teachers, the parents or should society decide through some kind of centralized control? These are questions which we have touched upon already and which we must take up again in later chapters.

One point must be made here, however, which is crucial. Whoever does take these decisions or does contribute to them must be encouraged to realize the slender nature of the foundations on which any system of values or set of criteria he is using will be based. His choices should, therefore, be tentative and of such a kind as to avoid dogmatism. Furthermore, they should be open to continuous evaluation and modification since that is the essence of curriculum development. If knowledge were God-given and if values enjoyed a similar status, then curriculum development could have only one meaning as the slow progression towards perfection that Plato had in mind. Such a notion is surely no longer tenable.

Summary and conclusions

We have considered in this chapter some of the arguments put forward for the inclusion of particular subjects or particular kinds of content in the curriculum from three perspectives — views of the nature of society and of culture, epistemological theories of the nature of knowledge and ideas that have been expressed about the nature of children and ways in which a consideration of this can be the central concern of curriculum planning. We then considered some of the problems of establishing a framework of values within which choices of curriculum content could be made, concluding that such a framework must be recognized as subjective and, as a result, highly tentative.

We must end this discussion of curriculum content by recognizing that in practice we shall, as teachers, make decisions about the content of the work of each of our pupils by reference to all of the criteria that the theorists offer us. We will be concerned with theories of knowledge, although, as we have seen, this may be the least useful source of advice to teachers or curriculum planners; we will be concerned with society in terms of its general needs and any common culture we feel we can identify; and we will pay due regard to the individual needs, interests and experience of each child in so far as we feel we can identify them. In fact, as is so often the case, the oppositions and polarities exist more in the minds of curriculum theorists than in the realities of curriculum practice.

Furthermore, in reaching these decisions we shall all display a degree of subjectivity that is only to be expected in any human activity. This subjectivity must be recognized and accepted if we are to achieve a proper perspective for our curriculum planning. The main fault with all or most of the theories we have looked at is that they represent attempts to achieve some kind of objective basis for decisions about curriculum content and this, as I have tried to show, is an impossibility. The very idea itself of curriculum *development* implies that we are not dealing with an issue which will be productive of hard and fast answers, unless we see it, again like Plato, as a progression towards some ideal state. The notion of development implies continuous reappraisal and change and, therefore, suggests that we should not be searching for some once-for-all, God-given criteria but rather accepting the idea that any criteria we find will themselves be continuously evolving, so that decisions we make about the content of our pupils' work will inevitably be based on our own subjective judgements of those criteria and their impact and import.

Lastly, let us remember too that there is room in the working week for many different kinds of activity, each perhaps justified by reference to different kinds of consideration (James 1968). Schools fulfil many purposes and not all of these purposes can be attained by one kind of activity. Our concern here has been with arguments that purport to justify the inclusion of certain kinds of curriculum content on educational grounds. But, as we suggested at the beginning of this chapter, education is not the only concern of the school. Schooling embraces a good deal more. Many decisions that we make, therefore, concerning the content of our pupils' work will be made not by reference to educational arguments but after consideration of such things as our pupils' social or vocational requirements. It is important to remember this so that we are not tempted to exclude activities on the grounds that their main justification is not an educational one. Again we have Plato to thank for this dichotomy between the liberal and the vocational, the theoretical and the practical, and it is time he was pensioned off.

This is not to say on the other hand that we should not endeavour at the same time to ensure that all activities are, as far as is possible, educational in the broad sense. It is rather to accept that many kinds of justification are possible, so that the whole process of planning the content of any curriculum is a good deal more complex than some of the arguments we have been considering would suggest. Again in the last analysis it all rests with the professional judgement of the individual teacher. The most that we can hope, therefore, is that that judgement is truly professional, in other words, that while being subjective it is also informed and firmly based on a full knowledge and understanding of the issues involved. It is to help teachers to develop that knowledge and understanding as a basis for the crucial decisions they must make that this chapter, and indeed this book, has been written.

CHAPTER 4

CURRICULUM INTEGRATION

Demands that the curriculum be made relevant, meaningful and so on have been the most potent factor in the development of the idea of curriculum integration, one of the most significant features of curriculum development and change in the United Kingdom over the last ten years or so. This is the direction in which many teachers have felt it appropriate to develop the curriculum, in spite of the fact that the most influential educational philosophers have been first of all asserting it to be logically impossible and later searching without real success for the logical and espistemological basis upon which it has been accomplished. It is a development which more clearly than any other illustrates the problems of curriculum content which we discussed in the last chapter.

The most interesting feature of this phenomenon is the fact that it has ever been seen as a serious problem. That it has been so viewed has been in the main a result of looking at the questions it raises from the point of view of one particular theory of knowledge. Curriculum integration, even in the terms of that particular theory of knowledge, has been with us for years. For man has always integrated his knowledge as he has focused it on certain concerns that have been important to him. It is only because people have felt it necessary to refocus knowledge in order to deal with new concerns that the problem of integrating hitherto separate areas of knowledge has been raised. Clearly it is a problem, since it raises certain practical difficulties for school organization; but it is not a logical problem since, if it were, either we would have been aware of it long ago or we should by now have encountered real difficulties in dealing with long-existing kinds of integrated knowledge such as the study of geography. 'How can the curriculum be integrated?' is thus to some a question rather like 'Have you stopped beating your wife?' since it is only meaningful if one accepts as true the assumptions that lie behind it.

Forms of knowledge

The source of the logical difficulties that it is claimed the integration of the curriculum raises is to be found in a theory of knowledge which regards knowledge as organized into several logically discrete forms of knowledge, forms of understanding (Hirst 1965) or realms of meaning (Phenix 1964). It is this initial assumption about knowledge that creates the difficulty, since clearly, if these bodies of knowledge are different from each other in their logical structure, it will be not merely difficult but downright impossible to integrate them in any real sense.

In an issue as central to recent curriculum planning as this, it is important to be absolutely clear about the point that is being made here. It is not a matter of knowledge being divided up into *subjects* that we are concerned with; it is the existence of logical differences between kinds of knowledge, which leads us to recognize their existence as separate *disciplines*. How crucial this distinction is will become apparent later.

There are four main aspects to the logical differences that it is being claimed distinguish each of these forms of knowledge from the others. Firstly, each form has 'certain central concepts that are peculiar in character to the form. For example, those of gravity, acceleration, hydrogen and photosynthesis characteristic of the sciences; number, integral and matrix in mathematics; God, sin and predestination in religion; ought, good and wrong in moral knowledge.' (Hirst 1965, p. 129). These concepts are of course sometimes used in the context of other forms of knowledge but in a rational structure of knowledge these concepts fall naturally into one particular form.

Secondly, each form has its own distinctive logical structure. A systematic body of knowledge consists of networks of relationships through which experience is understood and these networks fall into several categories, such as mathematics, the physical sciences, the human sciences, literature and fine arts, morals, religion and philosophy. Each of these networks of relationships, it is claimed, is of a distinct logical kind from the others. There is of course overlap, as between, for example, mathematics and the physical sciences, but the fact that there is overlap does not imply that important logical differences do not exist.

Thirdly, each form has its own distinctive truth criteria, its own method of validating the assertions it consists of. Mathematical assertions, for example, are to be verified by procedures that are quite different from those that are used to verify scientific assertions and there are further different verification procedures, each appropriate and peculiar to a particular form of knowledge.

Lastly, each form has its own distinctive methodology. Each has its own 'particular techniques and skills for exploring experience' (Hirst 1965, p. 129). Each form therefore represents a different set of procedures for extending human knowledge and experience in the area with which it is concerned.

Such an analysis of human knowledge, as we noted in Chapter 3, provides a clear-cut basis for curriculum planning in that it indicates seven or eight distinct forms of rationality into which, it is claimed, the developing rational mind must be initiated. It also, however, creates problems whenever we feel for any reason that some form of integration of knowledge is necessary or desirable. We must be quite clear, however, about exactly what these problems are and how far-reaching they are since a good deal of confusion is apparent both in what is said about the integration of knowledge and what in practice is done about it.

The integration of knowledge

In the first place, we must again remind ourselves that no logical problems are created when we wish to integrate subjects but only when the integration of separate disciplines is involved. The development of what is being called 'integrated science' does not raise logical problems since all the subjects to be integrated fall within the same form of knowledge. Often the problems that face those wishing to develop some kind of integrated studies programme are administrative rather than logical, the term integration being used in this case not to indicate the need to put two or more logically different forms of knowledge together but merely (although often this proves to be a greater problem) to get two or more departments or university boards of studies to work together. Thus, in a particular context a subject such as nutritional studies might not be seen in itself as a form of integrated study, which on this kind of analysis of knowledge it clearly is, but the integration of this with, say, home economics would be regarded as presenting problems of integration. We must be clear that the problems such developments create are entirely administrative; logical difficulties either do not exist since all are branches of the same discipline, as in the case of integrated science, or they have already gone unnoticed, as in the development of an integrated field such as nutritional studies.

Secondly, we must also not lose sight of the fact that not all attempts to put subjects, or even disciplines, together will raise problems of integration. Certainly not all will raise epistemological problems. It is possible to devise integrated studies programmes — and there are many such about — in which no attempt is made to do any more than to develop related kinds of content in each subject area, to try to achieve, for example, more point to a geological study of the British Isles by linking it to an historical study of the development of forms of physical communication. The intention here is not that the content of each element should be interwoven into one complete 'whole', but merely that each should be related to the other.

Similarly, some programmes offer a choice of activities to pupils which include several subjects and span several disciplines, but the actual work each pupil does is within rather than across disciplines. Such programmes are multi-disciplinary rather than genuinely inter-disciplinary and do not therefore generate the logical difficulties that have caused some people such concern. Only when it is intended that the different packages of knowledge should be welded into one do we have an apparent logical problem and only here, if anywhere, is there a need to develop an interdisciplinary logic.

Thirdly, before we become too dismayed at the prospect of having to develop such an interdisciplinary logic, let us remember that it has already been done with apparent success. Many of the subjects that stand unquestioned on the curricula of schools, colleges and universities are forms of integrated study; they are *fields* of knowledge rather than *forms* of knowledge, *subjects* rather than *disciplines*. Geography, drawing on mathematics, the physical sciences and the human sciences, is perhaps the most immediately obvious example of this, as we have already noted, but there are many others — domestic science, physical education, design and technology studies, comparative education and, indeed, the study of education itself. Nothing reveals the confusion of thinking that has been characteristic of this area more clearly than the problems some people are prepared to find in integrating, say, health education with education studies generally, while being unaware of and unable to give any account of the problems that on their own analysis must already have been overcome in integrating mathematics, the physical sciences, the human sciences and moral knowledge to form the area of study known as health education itself, in the first instance.

If the integration of disciplines creates logical problems then it must also create them for those attempts at integration that took place before the notion of logically discrete forms of knowledge was first mooted, just as much as for those attempts that have been made since. Alternatively, if such subjects have solved the logical difficulties, then it should not be difficult for us to find similar solutions for new forms of integration. In fact, the whole issue continues to appear to be a non-problem or at least a problem created, as we commented at the outset, by too close an adherence to a particular theory of knowledge.

Reasons and purposes

We must now ask why it is that, in spite of the administrative difficulties and the stated logical problems, so many teachers in schools, colleges and universities have wanted to undertake the chore of developing new forms of integrated studies.

There are at least two different, although both practically and theoretically interrelated, reasons for this, two kinds of purpose that teachers have had in embarking on such a course. What they have in common is that they both represent an attempt to develop a curriculum from a consideration of factors other than those deriving from beliefs about the nature of knowledge. In other words, they lend support to the claim that has already been made that the main thrust of recent curriculum development has rightly been towards seeking justification for curricular decisions from sources other than those of philosophy in general or epistemology in particular, and they add strength to the assertion we made in Chapter 3 that epistemological considerations in themselves have little if anything that is positive to contribute to curriculum planning.

In the first place, we have what we might call a psychological reason for curriculum integration. As we suggested at the beginning of this chapter, many people have looked towards some form of integration as a possible solution to some of the problems raised by the apparent rejection by many pupils of the content of their education. We have already referred to notions such as that of the alienation of pupils from the curriculum, the absence of any kind of interest or source of motivation, the feeling that there is little relevance in what schools are offering. For these reasons, as we saw in Chapter 3, many have recommended that we should start curriculum planning from a consideration, not of the nature of knowledge, but of the needs and interests of the pupils. Others have looked to a complete change of methods, to the idea of promoting pupil enquiry rather than proceeding entirely through a teacher-dominated didacticism. Either or both of these devices have been seen as likely to enhance motivation and to ensure therefore a higher level of work and achievement. One slightly worrying feature of this kind of development has been that it has often been confined to the curriculum planned for the less able pupil where the problems of motivation and, indeed, of control of behaviour have been most apparent. However, this factor provides further evidence that this has been a major purpose of many schools and teachers in introducing these new approaches to the planning of their curriculum.

It is of course possible to pursue both interest-based and enquiry-based methods within existing subjects and many situations can be found in which this is done, not least those in which such schemes as the Nuffield science projects are being operated. It will be apparent, however, that it is not easy to confine children's interests or their enquiries within particular subject boundaries, so that if we wish to pursue seriously these particular methods some form of integrated studies programme will often inevitably follow. This has been the experience of many schools where the improvement of the children's response to the school has been the main purpose behind the introduction of integrated studies programmes of various kinds.

The second reason for the introduction of some form of curriculum integration, although closely related to the first, is sociological rather than psychological. Some curriculum content can appear and can actually be irrelevant to pupils not only because they do not see the point of it but because it has no point. Conversely, some areas of knowledge which do have point and relevance do not appear on the curriculum because they do not fit the discipline or subject categories traditionally reflected there.

This is one respect of a wider feature of human knowledge which we must recognize. We have already noted that some areas of knowledge are not characterized by being logically discrete forms but by being fields of knowledge, issues of importance around which different bodies of knowledge tend to cohere or become organized. Thus, as we have noted several times, geography is a field of knowledge which focuses several different kinds of knowledge on the issue of man and his environment. Traditional groupings of subjects will therefore represent those areas of knowledge that had value and importance when these groupings were made. A changing society will inevitably create new bases for the organization of knowledge and these will require that the traditional forms of organization, whether of subjects or disciplines, be changed constantly and continuously to meet the changing needs.

An interesting example of this kind of reorganization and regrouping of subjects is that which is taking place in that area of the curriculum that was once called 'handicraft' through the linking of design studies with science and technology to form 'design and technology', a new and very different curriculum subject (Hicks 1976). Clearly, this development is to a large extent a response to the kinds of pressure we are discussing to restructure knowledge to meet changing social needs.

Teachers have been aware also that many of the issues that appear to be important and relevant to children growing up in present-day society fall neither into the disciplines nor into the subject categories of the traditional school curriculum. In fact they often fall right through the gaps. Live issues in most spheres straddle the boundaries between the disciplines and, while they continue to be live, they require a constant re-organization of knowledge. One of the best examples of this has been the Schools Council's Humanities Curriculum Project which, in endeavouring to encourage senior pupils in secondary schools to explore topics of crucial interest and concern to them as members of contemporary society, topics such as relations between the sexes, law and order, living in cities, war and so on, quickly discovered that such topics could not be dealt with adequately within any traditional subject area but would necessarily involve some kind of interdisciplinary development. Similarly, recent years have also seen the emergence of other kinds of humanities course, as we have come to recognize that many or all of the subjects normally subsumed under that heading can profitably be pursued together as all contributing to our understanding of man. This has, therefore, been a prime reason for the introduction of new forms of integrated studies in our schools.

One direct implication that should be noted here is that it requires that any attempt at curriculum integration should be centred on an organizing theme or concept that is properly meaningful. The idea of using a theme to unite the various contributions to an integrated programme or enquiry has been a popular one, not least because it provides a manageable framework within which both teachers and pupils can work. Sometimes, however, the themes are tenuous in the extreme as in the, probably apocryphal, example of the theme 'Hands' being used to focus the integration of biology (the physical structure of hands), industrial sociology (working with one's hands) and religious studies (the 'laying-on of hands') or in the example Lawrence Stenhouse gives of the theme 'Water' being used to link irrigation, boiling kettles, swimming and water on the knee (Stenhouse 1969). If we are to justify the introduction of new combinations of subjects and areas of knowledge on the grounds that such reorganization is necessary to meet changing social needs or to ensure that learning has meaning and relevance for the pupil, then those new combinations cannot be arbitrary collections of subject matter but must have some central focus such as is provided by the controversial issues of the Humanities Curriculum Project. In short, they must represent changes in the organization of knowledge that are meaningful both in social terms and to the individual pupil.

Other theories of knowledge

These natural changes in the organization of human knowledge and the corresponding developments in the curriculum do not always raise serious logical problems since often the problems they raise are not epistemological but merely administrative, as we noted above in the case of such developments as integrated science courses.

For some, however, they do not raise such problems even when integration of disciplines seems to be involved, since, as we have seen, many do not accept the existence of these logical distinctions in the first place but regard all knowledge as one and indivisible. We have already examined in some detail John Dewey's view that all knowledge is ultimately reducible to the form of scientific knowledge, the results of that experimentation we constantly engage in to resolve the problems presented by all aspects of our human environment, not only the physical aspects but also the social, cultural, aesthetic and moral.

If one accepts that kind of view of knowledge then integration of subjects will present us with no logical problems at all. In fact, on this sort of view we will start by seeing knowledge as undifferentiated, in the way that on the whole most primary schools do, and accept that subject divisions will only emerge in the later stages of formal education and then only when they have point for the learner in the organization of his own knowledge. Furthermore, the divisions that appear even then will not be of a logical kind; they will represent the organization of knowledge into convenient fields on the basis of social and personal relevance and will acknowledge the need for constant change, re-organization and reappraisal of these fields. In short, we will accept that the way in which the adult generation has structured its knowledge will not necessarily continue for ever to be the most satisfactory structure for subsequent generations and the need to plan for constant integration and reintegration of knowledge will be acknowledged. Such a notion has been criticized as representing an instrumental view of knowledge, but it is difficult to understand what knowledge is if it is not to be instrumental to man's purposes either individually or collectively.

This is of course one particular aspect of that view that sees education as being essentially a matter of the developing experience of the individual. If relevance is to mean anything in relation to the content of the curriculum, or conversely, if alienation is to be avoided, then as Whitehead told us a long time ago we must avoid 'inert knowledge' (Whitehead 1932). In other words, we must put the pupil in a situation in which he can organize his knowledge in ways that are meaningful to him as well as to society. This is the point of those claims that are made that education be seen as a dialectical relationship between the pupil and his environment (James 1968) or that it should be concerned with the intentions that lie behind the conscious activity of the pupil (Freire 1972) or that it should be seen as an extension of the 'common-sense knowledge' that the pupil brings to the teaching situation (Keddie 1971).

In brief, the epistemological basis for all such views is one that accepts that knowledge is instrumental and denies the 'out-there', God-given, objective nature of human knowledge, regarding all knowledge as subjective, as socially constructed, as 'a product of the informal understandings negotiated among members of an organized intellectual collectivity' (Blum 1971, p. 117) or which even takes the phenomenologist's completely personalized view.

A second, and perhaps largely negative, reason for rejecting this theory of knowledge as divided into logically discrete forms, and therefore not recognizing any fundamental difficulties in the notion of curriculum integration, is the fact that no really clear account has yet been given of what constitutes the differences between the forms of knowledge, other than that between the logical/mathematical and the empirical/scientific forms, a distinction which is itself open to debate. It is one thing to assert that seven or eight different species of knowledge exist; it is quite another to give an account of the logical form of each. Until such an account can be given it is perhaps unwise to take on trust the existence of such divisions and particularly to base far-reaching curricular decisions on them. There is also the related fact that we can observe that much of human knowledge, as we keep on asserting, has been organized quite effectively and without difficulty in an inter-disciplinary way. This must lend support to the argument that knowledge is socially constructed or at least organized to achieve certain social purposes and therefore to the view that the main appeal of curriculum planning should be to sociological considerations.

If, nevertheless, we wish to cling to the view that there are logically discrete forms of knowledge while at the same time recognizing, as we must, the need for the organization of knowledge also into fields, then we have indeed got a logical difficulty to resolve. Furthermore, the same kinds of logical consideration would seem to suggest that to find a solution to this difficulty must be a logical impossibility, if the logical differences are as marked as is being claimed. For to argue that we must seek for an interdisciplinary logic that will enable us to operate between or across forms of knowledge (Hirst and Peters 1970) is to suggest that it is possible to find a form of logic that will enable us to achieve some kind of unity of knowledge. This in turn would seem to imply firstly that the logical differences between the forms are not as hard and fast as we have been encouraged to believe and, secondly, that we might be more profitably engaged in seeking for this form of logic that will weld knowledge together rather than in continuing the search for those forms which create problems for us when we want to organize our knowledge to some useful but novel end.

The alternative solution that has been offered to this problem of integrating discrete disciplines is no more satisfactory since it seems to beg the whole question. It has been suggested that we can plan the curriculum in terms of certain groupings of subjects, broad fields of experience, such as the practical subjects, the humanities, mathematics and the sciences (Newsom Report) or 'cores', such as mathematics, the sciences, the humanities, the expressive arts and moral education (Lawton 1973).

While this kind of approach may well make practical sense and may result in resolving some of the problems of alienation, relevance and so on that we have been considering, it certainly begs the epistemological question. For in telling us, probably quite rightly, that we should concentrate on fields of knowledge, it is not providing us with any kind of logical argument for integration but rather again asserting the sociological case. To claim that in the case of the humanities, for example, there is a conceptual unity which transcends the boundaries of the disciplines is not to solve the logical problem — rather it is to compound and confuse it; it is also to fail to recognize that what holds them together is that they constitute a field of knowledge focused on a central concern — man.

Such views, in other words, tell us yet again that there are strong sociological arguments for integration but they do not begin to deal with any of the logical problems that such arguments may raise. The theories are not necessarily themselves in error, but they are incompatible with theories about the existence of logically discrete bodies of knowledge.

Social and political implications

The fact that we constantly return to the social and sociological sources of justification for the organization of knowledge within the curriculum should alert us to the need to examine some of the social and political implications that it has been claimed curriculum integration has. It is to this aspect of curriculum integration that we must now turn.

'How a society selects, classifies, distributes, transmits and evaluates the educational knowledge it considers to be public, reflects both the distribution of power and the principles of social control' (Bernstein 1971, p. 47). If this is so, then a major change such as the move towards different forms of integration that we are discussing must itself reflect changes in the distribution of power and principles of social control in contemporary society. What sorts of change are being reflected?

It has been posited (Bernstein 1967, 1971) that this move from a curriculum in which the subject boundaries are relatively fixed and strong, a 'collection code', to one in which the boundaries are wide and there is a trend towards increased integration, an 'integrated code', is one aspect of a more general trend in education towards 'open' rather than 'closed' schools, towards a mixing of categories, towards diversity rather than purity, and that this is symptomatic of basic changes in the culture of our society, particularly changes in the principles of social control (Bernstein 1967), in short, a corresponding move from a 'closed' to an 'open' society, from what Durkheim has called mechanical solidarity to what he called organic solidarity. Hitherto knowledge has been seen as dangerous and needing to be confined to certain people; the different categories of knowledge must be well insulated from each other, since the results of admixtures are difficult to predict; specialization, it is claimed, makes knowledge safe and therefore helps to maintain the social order; the transmission of knowledge is best left in the control of the teacher. Integration, involving education in breadth, threatens the principles of social order; it weakens the authority systems of society; it represents a move away from a society in which the form of social integration is mechanical, based on a shared system of values and assigned social roles, a 'closed' society, to one in which the form of social integration is organic, that is, a society which is pluralist, tolerating many different value systems, in which social roles are achieved and in which, therefore, social integration arises out of differences between individuals, an 'open' society.

These are some of the social implications that have been found in a move within the school and especially within the curriculum from a collection to an integrated code, from purity of categories to diversity, from a concern with pure knowledge to a concern with its application, from education in depth to education in breadth, from specialization which stresses difference to generalization which stresses commonality.

This same trend therefore results in similarly far-reaching changes in the social order of the school. In the first place, it has immediate implications for the hierarchy of order and control within the school, for teachers' relationships with each other and for their roles. When sub-ject boundaries are strongly maintained, the organization of the institution remains firmly in the hands of the head and the heads of the subject departments; individual staff members are for the most part only involved professionally within their departments. Thus strong subject loyalties are maintained. A move towards an integrated code will challenge this loyalty, threaten the departmental base and, therefore, materially alter the relationships between teachers, since they must now learn to work together, to cooperate with each other across subject departments. This in turn is likely to lead to changes in the hierarchy of the institution and a major shift in its power base; decisions will be reached by different procedures and individual teachers will be more closely involved in them; indeed, it is likely also to lead to situations in which the need for the participation of the pupils or students themselves in decision making will be recognized.

Important changes are likely to take place too in what will count as knowledge in such an institution. We have already referred to the distinction to which sociologists are currently drawing our attention between educational knowledge and common-sense knowledge. A collection code will tend to be largely concerned with educational knowledge since, as we have seen, it has been suggested that such a code will be concerned more with pure than with applied knowledge. It will tend also to see knowledge as some 'out-there' God-given entity rather than as the product of human endeavour. A move towards an integrated code will represent a move towards recognizing the man-made nature of knowledge and towards including common-sense knowledge in the curriculum. Indeed, as we saw above, this is borne out by the fact that many teachers justify the adoption of an integrated curriculum in terms of its increased relevance and its relation to the pupil's own experience. For the same reason, we have already noted the tendency to introduce such curricula initially for the benefit of the less able pupils and we may note here this added indication of its connection with social control.

Thirdly, a point which follows closely on what we have just said, such a development has important implications for attitudes towards knowledge and especially the attitudes of pupils towards it. 'Knowledge under collection is private property . . . . Children and pupils are early socialized into this concept of knowledge as private property. They are encouraged to work as isolated individuals with their arms around their work' (Bernstein 1971, p. 56). Again an integrated code brings with it a more open attitude to knowledge and to its acquisition. The emphasis is much more on collaboration and sharing of knowledge, cooperation ceases to be 'cheating' and becomes acceptable and, as a result, the whole substance of inter-pupil relationships is changed.

This in turn will have its impact on the authority structure of the institution and in particular on the relationships between teacher and taught. In a school in which a relatively fixed view of knowledge holds sway, in which it is seen as something external to be acquired and in which the boundaries between subjects are strongly maintained, the relationships between teachers and pupils will tend to be distant, largely formal and impersonal and the authority structure hierarchical, clear-cut and for the most part positional, the teacher deriving his authority more from the fact that he has been set *in* authority than that he is *an* authority. Where his expertise is relevant it will be that expertise that he has as an authority in a particular subject area. Tradition will also play its part in helping the teacher to establish his authority in this kind of school (Hargreaves 1972).

In a school which takes the view of knowledge and of education that we have seen to be implicit in an integrated code, teacher-pupil relationships will have to be more personalized, since the teacher will be less distant from the pupil. Position and tradition will not offer much support to the development of authority. A much greater premium will be placed on being *an* authority, on possessing expertise, and that expertise will need to embrace a wider range of pedagogic skills than mere knowledge of a subject area.

This kind of analysis of what is involved in a move towards curriculum integration has been offered as an objective, descriptive outline of some of its implications. In view of what it reveals, however, it is not surprising that this kind of development has been deplored by some people both within the teaching profession and outside it, nor that it has met with a good deal of opposition at all levels. Some of these objections have come from those who, like the contributors to Black Papers, appear to be opposed to any change in education, except perhaps a return to the practices of former times, and who must therefore be assumed to be of the opinion that current educational practices or traditional methods are wholly right. The opposition of some teachers can be put down to the fact that change of this kind or, indeed, of any kind in schools brings with it many practical difficulties of a kind that some teachers are unwilling to invite too readily; some of these we must consider shortly.

Before we do so, however, we must look briefly at some theoretical objections that have been raised to curriculum integration and its social implications

It has been claimed that subject specialization is one instance of the division of labour and that this is our only defence against centralized autocracy (Musgrove 1973). In other words, integration is seen as introducing sameness into the curriculum and therefore as likely to lead to centralized control and a loss of that very pluralism that is seen as essential to the integration of society. The concept of organic solidarity, as defined by Durkheim, is again used here but this represents a totally different application of that concept to the school situation from that of Basil Bernstein, by whom the move towards integration was seen as one aspect of the move towards organic solidarity rather than away from it.

Similarly, it has been argued that within the school or any educational institution this development is likely to lead to a loss of power by individuals and that it should be seen therefore as an attack on departments and the power of their heads and as a step towards increased autocracy for head teachers, principals and vice-chancellors (Musgrove 1973). This again represents a totally different analysis of the situation rather than opposition to what others have seen as the main thrust of integration, that is, towards increased individuality and diversity and therefore away from centralization of control and homogeneity of values. It is difficult therefore to understand how it can be claimed at the same time that the integrated curriculum is in the last resort a prescription for social anarchy. Either it leads to tighter centralized control or to anarchy but it surely cannot lead to both. This amounts therefore not so much to a criticism of integration as perhaps to a misinterpretation of its implications.

It has also been argued that integration with its eroding of boundaries between specialist subjects will lead to a loss of structure to pupils' learning and a loss of quality in learning, that subject categories are necessary to bring order into children's learning and that quality of educational experience can only be maintained if teachers can develop expertise in a narrow area of knowledge (Musgrove 1973). There are several points that need to be made in reply to this.

In the first place it fails to recognize that the whole thrust of the movement towards integration has been prompted as we have seen by a desire to introduce more order and structure, more meaning and relevance into children's learning, but that it has at the same time recognized the importance of endeavouring to ensure that that order and structure should be the child's order and structure and that it should therefore have meaning and relevance for him.

Secondly, there would seem to be no basis for the assumption that an integrated curriculum necessarily leads to the erosion of specialisms or to any loss of rigour or quality of learning. Indeed, one of the main points of the particular brand of integration that Goldsmiths' College pioneered under the name of IDE, Interdisciplinary Enquiry, has been that a return to a generalist approach in teaching must be avoided and that a prime need of any integration of disciplines is that it should be done by teachers who have, if anything, a greater expertise in their subject areas rather than a lesser, since greater understanding of what one's subject has to offer in the total education of the child becomes necessary as soon as one sets about attempting to integrate it with other subjects. Furthermore, as we have seen, certain versions of curriculum integration are the result of a need that has been felt to reorganize and restructure knowledge to meet new and changed purposes. There is no reason to believe that such new subjects as emerge need reveal any less rigour than those they replace and there is certainly no basis for the assumption that existing subject groupings have status that they must maintain for all time, regardless of diminishing relevance, of social change or of change of any other kind. We are here back to views of knowledge as a God-given entity.

Thirdly, this kind of criticism assumes that curriculum integration is a single thing and fails to recognize that there are almost as many kinds of integrated curricula as there are schools practising integration. Like all other forms of curriculum innovation, curriculum integration takes its character in each case from the particular requirements and features of the context in which it is to be found (Warwick 1973). As we have seen, there are a number of different purposes or reasons that teachers might have in introducing programmes of this kind so that the particular form in which they emerge in each situation will vary according to those reasons and purposes. Thus there are schemes in which the academic content of each contributory discipline is very carefully fixed and structured by the specialist department or teacher responsible for it, while there are others in which the individual child has almost unlimited freedom of choice. Sometimes the methods are largely heuristic; sometimes a good deal of direct instruction is employed of a completely didactic kind. There are some schemes in which teachers are encouraged to adopt a 'generalist' approach; there are many others, again like Goldsmiths' IDE, which hinge on a pattern of team-teaching in which each teacher contributes as a specialist. One can also find almost every possible permutation of subject involvement according to such basic local factors as the consideration of which departments have heads who believe in integration or are prepared to accept the extra work that will be involved in getting it off the ground. Thus we hear of integrated science schemes, integration of various combinations of humanities subjects with the addition sometimes of one or more of the expressive arts, and occasionally schemes which attempt to combine all kinds of subject. Each form of integration will present its own problems; not all will present epistemological problems, as we have seen, but each will have to be looked at on its own merits. There is so much variety that it is not possible to generalize.

For this reason, the Schools Council's Integrated Studies Project set out not to promote one distinctive form of integrated curriculum but rather to explore the range of possibilities this approach offered, to provide guidelines for teachers and to supply them with materials and ideas that they could adapt to their own purposes and to suit their own particular needs (Schools Council 1972b). In other words, it 'did not aim to provide a teacher-proof blueprint' (Shipman 1972, p. 147).

Lastly, we must note the dangers of the polarization that is implied by this kind of contrasting of subject-based and integrated curricula. Few secondary schools have adopted a totally integrated curriculum. Most include some form of integrated studies as only one aspect of a two- or three- or four-fold curriculum (James 1968). Nor is there anywhere where one can see an integrated code of a kind that can be contrasted so directly with a collection code. Basil Bernstein was speaking of ideal types not of realities. There are real dangers in using these ideal types as a basis for criticism of the practical realities of curriculum innovations which in themselves only loosely conform to them. There is very little in educational theory that can profit from the adoption of polarized stances of this kind. In most cases we should not be being invited to choose one extreme or another but rather to find a balance between them.

Practical problems

It is the enormous variety of integrated studies schemes that makes any detailed discussion of the practice of curriculum integration very difficult. Indeed, it should be a major consideration of every aspect of educational study which attempts to link theory to practice that every teacher's practice is his own and the most that we can do is to try to offer him theoretical considerations that will illuminate his own practice and enable him to develop a satisfactory theoretical perspective for himself. However, it must be remembered that those teachers who have been opposed to the introduction of forms of curriculum integration have usually based their criticisms on the practical difficulties they have experienced or have expected to experience rather than on abstruse theoretical arguments. We must try therefore to conclude this chapter with some consideration of the main kinds of practical problem that are likely to arise if some form of integration is undertaken.

Some of these practical aspects of curriculum integration have already emerged in our earlier discussion, particularly in relation to Basil Bernstein's analysis of its implications for the social order of the school. We must not lose sight of the risks to teachers from the possible loss of the identity and security that association with a particular subject gives them, if indeed this is going to be lost. On the other hand, it is perhaps salutary to note that this is a characteristic only of some teachers in secondary schools; teachers of younger children have for a long time had to find their professional identity and security in their pedagogic expertise and their understanding of aspects of child development and of the processes of education. Who is to say that it would be a bad thing if all teachers had to look towards such quarters for their professional status and security? Finally, we must not forget all of the effects of the changed relationships between teacher and teacher and especially between teacher and pupil that most forms of curriculum integration will bring about.

There are several other practical issues that we need to take cognisance of, however, and there is much to be said for considering these in some detail before embarking on any integrated studies programme. We must first get clear about the particular objectives of our scheme, our reasons and purposes in moving into this field and then we must look closely at our practical arrangements to ensure they are the best for achieving these purposes. Too often neither of these aspects is thought out clearly enough in advance so that quite pointless activities result, like some of the aimless project work that has brought this kind of work into general disrepute. The practical details must be thought out in relation to our aims and purposes and the following considerations are offered in the hope that they may help teachers with this planning or at least help them to avoid the worst pitfalls.

Integrated studies schemes usually raise problems for the organization of the school. Again, not all will do so, but those that involve increased freedom for pupils both in choice of work and of movement about the building, and those that involve a wider use of discovery techniques will raise particular problems of accommodation and timetabling.

Accommodation will need to be of a kind that will lend itself to these new purposes, workshops rather than traditional classrooms, and facilities will need to be provided for all of the activities it is envisaged pupils may be engaged in. Alternatively, it may be necessary for pupils to move to different kinds of room for different purposes and it will clearly be desirable in such cases for these rooms to be as close to each other as possible.

Most schemes of this kind will also necessitate major adjustments to the timetable. Subjects that are to be integrated will need to be timetabled together and a freer style of working will call for greater flexibility of organization and larger blocks of time than the normal 40—45-minute period. In practice, many schools have found that both flexibility and greater scope for sustained work can be provided by blocking time, that is, by allocating double periods or even full half-days to integrated studies programmes (Warwick 1973; Kelly 1974a), as is the normal practice in the primary school. Furthermore, such a solution makes the actual task of timetabling easier on the whole rather than more difficult once agreement of departments has been reached as to how much of their 'private' allocation of time is to be put into the pool for re-allocation in this way.

Again, most integrated studies programmes make demands on material resources of a kind that cannot easily be met from within the normal stock of books and equipment of the contributing departments. Much additional material and quite new kinds of resource have to be provided. Many teachers have found it helpful to produce work cards or work sheets of various kinds to guide pupils' work, but these need to be backed by sources to which pupils can refer in carrying out the tasks assigned to them or chosen by them. Furthermore, once this kind of material has been produced, it needs to be kept for future use, unless we are to find ourselves having to produce totally new material each time we deal with a certain topic or area of work. The production of new resources and the organization of an effective system of storage and quick retrieval become key tasks for teachers in this kind of situation (Kelly 1974a) and it is not advisable to enter any scheme of curriculum integration without giving some prior thought to questions of this kind.

The keeping of records also becomes of more importance if pupils are to be allowed greater freedom of choice in their work. It is no longer enough to remember what each class has covered; we need to know what each pupil has been engaged on. In part this has to be done to ensure that we can attend satisfactorily to the continuing educational development of each individual; it is also necessary, however, to allow for the fact that in any kind of school situation there will be some pupils who will attempt to find loop-holes in the system and will work on the same project and offer up more or less the same collection of work every time if we do not take steps to ensure that they cannot.

All of these organizational problems become more important if a system of team-teaching is also adopted (Lovell 1967; Freeman 1969; Warwick 1971; Kelly 1974a). Provision of suitable accomodation, proper timetabling, production of resources and the keeping of adequate records are even more necessary if the collaboration of several teachers is planned. In addition, it is vital that the team of teachers is able to meet regularly to plan and to exchange notes. Such regular meetings should be a formal feature of the timetable and should not be left to chance encounters over coffee, tea or lunch. Team-teaching has a great deal to offer in any educational situation but it is also fraught with many dangers and needs the most careful and elaborate planning and organization.

Team-teaching also highlights another aspect of the practical issues of curriculum integration which we have touched on before. If an integrated studies programme is to involve a totally new approach to teaching (and, unless it is, it may well not be worth venturing on it), it is going to create new roles for teachers and make new demands on their skills. Unless they are prepared to accept these new roles and develop these new skills, little good will come of it. A good deal of preliminary work is necessary, therefore, as with all curriculum innovations, both to persuade those teachers who are unconvinced of the advantages of the changes that are proposed, since to a large extent the success of any such venture will hinge on the attitudes of the teachers who are attending to it (Barker-Lunn 1970), and to help them to prepare adequately for the new work by producing the schemes of work, resources and so on they feel will be needed, by developing the new skills that will be required of them and by adopting the new attitudes required towards their professional tasks, their colleagues and their pupils. Much can be done and has been done by Teachers' Centres and other special in-service provision to meet these needs (Kelly 1975). In planning such preparation we must again never lose sight of the additional demands, especially on the relationships of teachers with each other, that team-teaching will make and of the new professional attitudes that teachers need to learn if they are to operate successfully within such schemes. Over a long period of time every teacher has become used to working in the isolation of his own carefully guarded territory; it is not easy, especially for the old dogs, to learn new tricks of cooperation, collaboration and sharing.

A final practical issue that we must refer to before closing this discussion of curriculum integration is the implication that it has for assessment generally and for public examinations in particular (Kelly 1974a, 1975). The whole question of the implications of assessment and examinations for curriculum development will be considered in detail in Chapter 6. It is enough here to note that curriculum integration poses special problems in this area. Several solutions have been found by teachers to meet these problems, but again this is an aspect of this kind of development that needs to be well thought-out in advance. New attitudes are needed to internal assessment and examination procedures but, more importantly, the external procedures must be available to match any such development. There are now public examinations at all levels in integrated studies of one form or another. For the most part these have been produced to answer the demands of teachers who were generating such programmes within their schools. This, of course, is the right order of procedures — curriculum innovation first and then the development of examination procedures to fit the new curriculum practices. But it is important when introducing any scheme to ensure either that the public examination system is already in a position to deal with it or to take the necessary steps to ensure that it will be in such a position by the time that one's first pupils are ready for it.

Summary and conclusions

We have examined some of the epistemological problems that it has been claimed are raised by attempts at curriculum integration and have suggested that epistemology, like all branches of philosophy, can do little more than attempt to clarify the questions for us and that there may be dangers in expecting it or allowing it to dictate answers, not least because different theories of knowledge quite clearly offer different answers. We then went on to suggest that it might be more profitable to examine the whole question of curriculum integration from a socio-logical point of view. In endeavouring to do this we discovered both certain kinds of rationale for curriculum integration and also some far-reaching political and social implications both for the internal societies of educational institutions themselves and for society at large. Finally, we considered some of the practical issues that are raised for schools and for teachers by such a development and suggested that these should be carefully thought-out against the background of a thorough theoretical understanding and in relation to the particular purposes of the individual institution if such a step is to be taken successfully and chaos and confusion avoided.

Curriculum integration does in fact create many administrative, practical and theoretical problems, but it only presents a logical problem if we take too rigid a view of knowledge and allow that view to dominate our approach to curriculum planning. If we do not, then we suddenly find that a good deal of curriculum integration has been with us for a long time. To extend this is to do no more than to accept that in any developing society the organization of knowledge must change and schools must produce pupils who can adapt and contribute to such changes. If schools are to do this, they must themselves be flexible, open to change and development, prepared to cope with the necessary organizational change and not tied too firmly to the past or to a fixed view of knowledge. As Dewey said, 'We live forward.'

This in fact is the general conclusion of the whole of our rather lengthy discussion of the nature of knowledge and its implications for the content of the curriculum. Questions about the nature of knowledge do raise a number of important issues for curriculum planners, some of which we have considered in some detail. But our discussions have led us always nearer to the conclusion that we must ultimately accept the 'man-made' and hypothetical nature of knowledge rather than try to maintain a mystical 'out-there' view. The strongest arguments for certain kinds of curriculum content, therefore, become those that are based on an appraisal of the needs of society and related sociological considerations.

Once the idea of social change is accepted, we see that this also implies the need for constant evaluation and reappraisal of the curriculum. Assertions about the curriculum must be seen as equally hypothetical and subject to change and development. Any theory of knowledge that does not allow for such change and development, indeed, any theory which does not have built-in devices for encouraging it, must be suspect and of doubtful value in an evolving situation. Continued and continuous curriculum development is necessary if the curriculum is to be a living organism rather than something that most pupils will reject as lacking any kind of vitality. Even if we agree, therefore, on certain forms of curriculum integration, such agreement will need to be only temporary and subject to continuous reassessment in the light of changing social and human needs.

Such continuous reassessment is central to the whole process of curriculum development and it can only be achieved if we can establish adequate procedures for the evaluation of what we do as a result of our curriculum planning. It is to a consideration of what that involves, therefore, that we must turn in our next chapter.

CHAPTER 5

CURRICULUM EVALUATION

We suggested in Chapter 1, when we were considering a number of models for curriculum planning, that evaluation might or might not be regarded as an essential component of such planning. It is certainly the case that many major curriculum innovations have not been accompanied by any attempt at evaluation. This was true of the many projects that were introduced both in Britain and in the U.S.A. in the late 1950s and early 1960s when public money was made available for curriculum development on a broader scale than had hitherto been possible. It seemed to be felt at that time that any curriculum change must be for the better. However, experience of later developments, particularly that which began to emerge as teachers in diverse school situations began to make many different uses of the projects and materials the developers presented them with, led to a gradual realization that evaluation had to be seen as an integral part of any curriculum *development*, so that in Britain arrangements for proper evaluation were made an essential requirement of all projects by such funding bodies as the Schools Council and every subsequent project had its own full-time evaluator (Hamilton 1976).

This process has more recently received another kind of support. For economic stringency has encouraged people to look even more closely at innovations that might prove expensive in order to ensure that they are fully justified. Furthermore, several events, such as those at the William Tyndale school, have raised a concern over standards of achievement by pupils and have led to public demand that teachers and other educationists should be made more clearly accountable to society for their decisions concerning the content and methods of their work. This clearly implies a closer monitoring of the work of the schools, particularly in the area of curriculum development.

Whatever the value of a central organization for the monitoring and evaluation of the work of the schools, it is difficult to argue against the notion that particular innovations need to be evaluated and that we need to assess very carefully the results of any change that we introduce. However, the sheer rapidity with which we have reached this awareness creates two kinds of difficulty for both the theory and the practice of curriculum evaluation.

In the first place, at least as far as Britain is concerned, this is the newest and, as a result, the most underdeveloped sector of curriculum theory, so that it is not only the most complex sector but also the most confused. Secondly, the recent rapid increase in the activities of evaluators in many different areas of the curriculum has led to the emergence of many new and different views of the nature and purposes of curriculum evaluation. Recent years have seen the appearance of a great diversity of curriculum projects and, therefore, a corresponding diversity of evaluation procedures (Schools Council 1973; Tawney 1975; Hamilton 1976). Both of these factors create difficulties for anyone attempting at this stage in the development of the art of curriculum evaluation to offer a coherent discussion of it or to give a clear and helpful overview of the current state of play.

These difficulties are compounded by the variety of purposes that one can have in making an evaluation of anything and the range of different conceptions one can have of such an activity, each of which may be perfectly suitable for some area of curriculum development. What might we be doing in evaluating a curriculum project? We might be doing no more than attempting to establish that the curriculum innovation is in fact happening, since we have already commented several times on the gap that often exists between the plans of the curriculum developer and the practice of the teachers supposedly implementing that curriculum project. On the other hand, we might be endeavouring to compare a particular project with other alternative methods, procedures or programmes in the same area. Is it really better than what it has replaced or than other new alternatives that are offered? Again, we might be concerned to do no more than to ascertain if it is acceptable to teachers and/or pupils (Schools Council 1974a). Then again, we might be attempting to reassure ourselves that we have got our objectives right or that our chosen procedures or content are right for the attainment of our objectives or that our objectives are being achieved and so on.

Everyone of these has been the main focus of the evaluation of at least one project and quite often several or all of them are built into the procedures adopted for the evaluation of any particular project. It is not possible, therefore, to provide a single useful definition of curriculum evaluation. It must vary according to the area of the curriculum we are dealing with, the curriculum model we have chosen and the purposes we have in mind when we set up our evaluation procedures. Such definitions of evaluation as are offered beg all or most of these questions, in so far as they represent a commitment to one or more particular views of evaluation (Harris 1963; Cronbach 1963; Wiley 1970; Stenhouse 1975). Furthermore, the term evaluation can describe many processes and can have many meanings; we can have many different aims in view when we set out to evaluate a curriculum, as we have just seen, and we can employ many different techniques in doing so; it can also be conducted by many different categories of people, some of whom will be concerned with its administrative function, others with its educational implications (Taba 1962).

We must note too that the questions to be asked in any process of evaluation are of at least two logically discrete kinds (White 1971). Some of them are empirical questions, which, like the investigations of a body such as the Consumers' Association, explore the relative merits of a project in terms of its costs, its effectiveness and so on. For questions of this kind we are looking, therefore, for relevant empirical data. Other questions, however, are asked in the process of evaluating a curriculum which are not of this kind but raise those difficult issues of value that we can never get far from in any discussion of education. These are the questions about ends rather than means, which ask whether the purposes of the activity are the right purposes, whether the experience being offered to pupils is of educational value, whether the curriculum is good in itself rather than merely effective in achieving its ends. Here the concern is to evaluate the goals of the curriculum itself and not merely the effectiveness of its procedures.

Thus there are many dimensions to curriculum evaluation so that the most sensible thing we can do would seem to be to begin by considering several types of curriculum evaluation or to consider some of the different dimensions of curriculum evaluation that people have identified.

Types of evaluation

It might be helpful first of all to note some general categories of evaluation. It is useful, for example, to distinguish in-course and post-course evaluation, those procedures that are designed to assess the work of the project as it proceeds and perhaps also to provide immediate feedback and those which are intended to be employed when the project is completed in order to assess its overall effectiveness. Another way of expressing this distinction, where the in-course procedures are intended to be used for continuous ongoing modifications, is to contrast 'formative' and 'summative' evaluation (Scriven 1967).

This is a distinction which reflects the differences of curriculum models we discussed in Chapter 1, since the simple classical linear curriculum model of objectives, content, procedures, evaluation clearly requires that the evaluation processes be 'summative', asking questions of a largely empirical kind, whereas the more sophisticated models involving continuous interchange between all four elements obviously demand evaluative procedures which are 'formative' and which will as a result be concerned at least in part with value questions. Such 'formative' evaluation will involve a number of dimensions, since it will be attempting both to assess the achievement of the objectives of the project and to discover and analyse barriers to the achievement of the goals (Stenhouse 1975). It may also be concerned to contribute to a modification of the objectives themselves, in short, to ask the 'value' questions we mentioned earlier.

We must also distinguish the evaluation of the curriculum itself from the assessment of the performance of individual students within it. Clearly these are again closely linked and interwoven and obviously the assessment of the performance of the students is one major source of data in the evaluation of the curriculum, but they are by no means the same, although many of the things that have been written about evaluation have tended to concentrate on the assessment of individual pupil performance.

It is perhaps worth noting, however, that assessment of the progress of individuals, except where it is concerned solely with end-of-course assessment, will involve a further type of 'formative' evaluation since the purpose now will be diagnostic of the difficulties that individuals are experiencing as a basis for modification of our method of treating them, for guidance and counselling generally. In other words, evaluation of this kind will be concerned to facilitate self-evaluation and feedback to pupils as well as teachers and curriculum planners (Wilhelms 1971).

Again we note that the variables are so many that this is a very difficult area to chart effectively. Several attempts have been made, however, to list the different possible types of curriculum evaluation. Thus Wynne Harlen, for example, has listed four types of evaluation 'which seem to have different purposes and functions in the main, though they overlap considerably' (Harlen 1971, pp. 128/9). First, 'evaluating the suitability of the objectives of an educational programme', in other words attempting to assess whether the objectives are worth trying to achieve and preferable to 'other possible and perhaps competing sets of objectives'. Secondly, 'on-going evaluation'; this is the 'formative' evaluation we have already referred to and 'has as its chief function helping the production of the educational programme once its objectives have been accepted'. Thirdly, 'evaluation of individual readiness and progress', which can be used by teachers themselves for such purposes as 'to diagnose their children's ability to benefit from certain experience, to gauge their progress, to locate their difficulties, and so on'. And fourthly, 'terminal or summative evaluation', the most important function of which is 'to find out whether the final product does, as a whole, achieve what it set out to do, whether it does this any better than other possible materials or approaches and how extended is any effect it may have' (Harlen 1971, pp. 128/9).

It is important to stress again that these divisions are largely conceptual, since several or all of them are likely to be involved in any one set of evaluation procedures in practice. Nor are they, therefore, to be seen as alternatives; each is likely to have its place at some stage in the development of any programme, according to the purposes of the planners (Harlen 1971). It is also worth noting here that the type of evaluation used will be closely tied to the curriculum model that has been adopted (Tawney 1973), as has become clear in the methods adopted by a number of varied Schools Council projects.

We must also acknowledge that a great deal of what has been said about evaluation both up to this point in this chapter and in other writings on the subject has tended to take for granted some kind of objectives model for curriculum planning and we must spend some time considering how far the prespecification of objectives is an essential prerequisite for the evaluation of a curriculum.

Evaluation and the prespecification of objectives

Early discussion of curriculum evaluation certainly tended to be fixed well within the context of the simple classical objectives model of the curriculum. Ralph Tyler, for example, is quite explicit on this point. 'The process of evaluation is essentially the process of determining to what extent the educational objectives are actually being realized by the program of curriculum and instruction' (Tyler 1949, pp. 105/6). And again, 'it is absolutely essential that they [the behavioural objectives] be defined in order to make an evaluation since unless there is some clear conception of the sort of behaviour implied by the objectives, one has no way of telling what kind of behaviour to look for in the students in order to see to what degree these objectives are being realized. This means that the process of evaluation may force persons who have not previously clarified their objectives to a further process of clarification. Definition of objectives, then, is an important step in evaluation' (Tyler 1949, p. 111).

A good deal of more recent discussion has also followed a similar line. The prespecification of objectives is made an explicit precondition for all the four types of evaluation listed by Wynne Harlen. The first activity that is involved in all of them, we are told, is 'clarifying objectives and analysing them to the point of expressing them in terms of behaviour changes' (Harlen 1971, p. 129). Nor is this surprising since she is writing from her experience of evaluating the Schools Council's Science 5-13 Project which, as we saw in Chapter 2, attempted to remain very firmly rooted in a classical objectives model. The evaluator, as a member of the project team, helped the team to clarify its behavioural objectives (Harlen 1971, 1973), which, as we saw in Chapter 2, were published in detail for the use of the teachers who were to use the project materials and implement the programme in their schools. The actual task of evaluation was then restricted to determining how far the teachers' guides that were produced enabled teachers to achieve these objectives and how they might be modified to increase their efficiency.

A good deal of both the theory and the practice of curriculum evaluation, therefore, has been set well within the context of an objectives-based curriculum model, and for this reason evaluation has been seen as centrally concerned to help with the framing and subsequent modification of objectives, the assessment of the suitability of the learning experiences to the achievement of the objectives set and the measurement of the degree to which the prestated objectives are being or have been attained. The need for proper accountability to which we have already referred also tends to encourage the use of this kind of model and it is relatively easy too with such a model to see the point and purpose of evaluation.

On the other hand, it is equally easy to recognize the dangers that lie in this kind of approach. For it is possible, and perhaps likely, that the kinds of evaluative procedure available will tend to govern or determine the choice of objectives, content or methods rather than merely to offer additional information to those selecting them on other grounds. We are all familiar with the teacher's everlasting complaint that the public examination syllabuses are the strongest determinants of the curriculum and the greatest inhibitors of curriculum change. Furthermore, we have already discussed at great length in Chapter 2 the difficulties and dangers that exist for curriculum planners in the view that all curriculum planning must start from a prespecification of objectives.

Thus, although there may seem to be a *prima facie* case for the pre-specification of objectives if adequate procedures of evaluation are to be found, we must pause to ask whether evaluation becomes quite impossible if we are not prepared to start with a statement of objectives and, if it does not, what differences does this necessitate in our methods of evaluation.

It might perhaps be worth beginning by dispelling the illusion that may have been created by what has been said so far that evaluation is an easy and straightforward matter when we work from a clear statement of objectives. For even here we face a number of difficulties, some of which derive from the unsuitability of this approach to certain areas of curriculum planning which we have already examined extensively in Chapter 2.

We have already referred to the temptation this approach offers to settle for those objectives whose achievement can easily be measured. The converse of this is the inability of current techniques of evaluation and assessment to measure the more sophisticated objectives teachers and educators adopt, especially in the affective domain (Kratwohl et al. 1964). As Schools Council Working Paper 26 tells us in discussing 'Education through the use of materials', 'a problem arises in assessing teaching that seeks to attain such objectives as "the development of desirable personality traits and attitudes" ' (Schools Council 1969a, p. 11). In other words, there exists a wide discrepancy between the scope of most sets of objectives and the scope of evaluation (Taba 1962) which will lead to inadequacies either in evaluation or in our specification of the objectives themselves.

Inadequacy of the available techniques of evaluation leads to further difficulties. At one level it can lead to conflict between the objectives made explicit by the project and those implicit in the evaluative techniques used (Taba 1962). Thus, no matter how far, for example, a project stresses its concern to develop pupils' understanding in a certain area of the curriculum, teachers will emphasize memorization and regurgitation of factual material if the main thrust of the evaluation procedures is towards this and better grades are obtained by those pupils who can reproduce learnt, but not necessarily assimilated, material most readily and in largest quantity. What is worse is that these procedures are often taken as indicators of the extent to which the real objectives of the programme have been attained so that a facility at repro-ducing scientific facts, for example, becomes confused with or is taken as evidence of the ability to think scientifically (Taba 1962).

On the other hand, if we succeed in avoiding this situation and make the somewhat inadequate techniques we have do a reasonable job of helping us to evaluate the more sophisticated objectives we may set our-selves, a good deal of interpretation of the data our evaluation procedures produce is still needed (Taba 1962). We need to measure against each other such things as memorization and understanding, knowledge and interest, achievement and social or educational back-ground, learning and psychological stages of intellectual and physical growth. The data our evaluation techniques produce, therefore, need to be interpreted against a broad backcloth and related to information from other sources and of other kinds, especially that coming from philosophical, psychological and sociological research. This is far from being a straightforward matter, so that even when objectives are clearly prespecified evaluation is not easy.

Furthermore, a proper evaluation requires a proper level of under-standing of the process that is being evaluated (Stenhouse 1975). A simple assessment of the attainment of objectives is concerned only with the success or failure of the programme; it is not concerned essentially with an understanding of it. It assesses without explaining (Stenhouse 1975). Thus the value of such evaluation is limited, since it can offer little feedback, if indeed it offers any at all, upon which the objectives or the procedures can be modified, so that it may well fail to do the very job it is designed to do. It is seldom helpful to know in black-and-white terms whether a project has succeeded or not. In fact, it will seldom be possible to make that kind of simple assessment. What is needed is a far greater complexity of data which can provide a basis for present and future curriculum development. This in turn implies the generation of evaluation procedures which do more than attempt to measure success or failure and which, in order to offer more, must be based upon a full understanding of the educational process itself.

Lastly, we must note that if we are dealing with an area of the curriculum or a kind of project for which the prespecification of objectives is inappropriate, any evaluation based on such a model will be equally inappropriate, will add to the confusion and may have quite disastrous consequences (Weiss and Rein 1969). One of those consequences we have already referred to several times, namely the tendency to modify the project to meet the assessment procedures being used. If we were right to argue in Chapter 2 that, at least for some areas of the curriculum such as the humanities or social education, an objectives model is not suitable, then any attempt to evaluate such projects in terms of what are thought to be their objectives must fail either by providing inadequate, unsatisfactory and irrelevant data or by persuading teachers to alter their approach to the work in such a way as to change its whole conception and scope.

On the other hand, to attempt no evaluation can be equally disastrous. This is well illustrated by the experience of those connected with the Goldsmiths' College development of Interdisciplinary Enquiry (IDE). Although a large number of schools were associated with this development and took it up with enthusiasm, no attempt was made to set up any formal scheme of evaluation. This was mainly due to the fact that no financial support was made available for what would have been an extremely expensive undertaking, although it was also in part a result of a conviction shared by most of the architects of the scheme that its value was self-evident. At all events, it was taken up or not taken up by schools and teachers according to their own private enthusiasms and convictions and it always lacked credibility in the eyes of its sternest critics, and especially those curriculum theorists who, quite rightly, felt it appropriate to ask for evidence of its effectiveness.

Hence others, who have been engaged in curriculum development for which they have felt the prespecification of objectives to be unsuited, have nevertheless recognized the necessity to design procedures by which it could be evaluated and have thus faced squarely the problems presented by the evaluation of a programme whose objectives cannot be stated in advance and whose evaluation procedures, therefore, must be based on a different, more sophisticated view of what the whole process of curriculum evaluation is. Certainly it would appear that a more sophisticated, developed view has begun to emerge from the work they have done.

Evaluation without prespecified objectives

The Schools Council's Integrated Studies Project which was set up at Keele University in 1968 had a brief which required it to consider a new way of organizing the curriculum rather than to measure the outcomes of pupils' learning in particular subjects, since its task was 'to examine the problems and possibilities of an integrated approach to humanities teaching in secondary schools' (Jenkins 1973, p. 70). Thus its concern was not to assess the extent to which certain purposes had been achieved but rather to evaluate the aims and purposes themselves of such an approach to the organization of the curriculum. To specify objectives at the beginning and to work on the production of materials designed to achieve those objectives was quite inappropriate.

The team, therefore, adopted a 'horizontal' curriculum model 'in which aims, learning experiences and material were developed concurrently' (Tawney 1973, p. 9). As a consequence of this, evaluation was seen not as a process for measuring the results of an experiment but as a device for continuously monitoring the project as it developed and constantly reviewing its aims, the packs of material that were produced and the practical problems that arose when it was introduced into schools. A major technique that was used was that of participant observation (Tawney 1973) and what emerged was not so much objective scientific data as a growing collection of experience and understanding of the issues and problems involved, which offered teachers therefore not a curriculum package as such but a set of principles and a body of knowledge to which they could refer and from which they might profit in developing their own schemes.

The most interesting project from the point of view of evaluation procedures, however, is the Humanities Curriculum Project, to which we have already referred on several occasions. We saw in Chapter 2 that this project has eschewed the idea of the prespecification of objectives more vigorously and more completely than any other. Being concerned to encourage pupils of secondary age to explore areas within the humanities and through discussion of all kinds to reach their own conclusions, the project team saw from the outset that to prespecify learning outcomes would be to contradict their own first principle and to beg the very questions they wanted to raise.

However, 'in an approach which is not based on objectives, there is no ready-made niche for the evaluator' (MacDonald 1973, p. 82). Furthermore, the team also felt it inappropriate to evaluate a curriculum project during its trial period so that, although Barry MacDonald, the project's evaluator — or Schools' Study Officer as he was significantly called — was appointed during the developmental stage of the project, his job was to prepare evaluation procedures for use after the project was firmly established in schools.

Both of these factors combined to present a particularly difficult set of problems in evaluation (Stenhouse 1975), difficulties which were acknowledged but which nevertheless were regarded as being there to be overcome. 'The evaluation then had to cope with an attempt at creative curriculum development with variable components, obvious disturbance potential and a novel approach' (MacDonald 1973, p. 83).

To meet these difficulties, Barry MacDonald adopted a 'holistic' approach. 'The aim of that stage [i.e. during the trial period] was simply to describe the work of the project in a form that would make it accessible to public and professional judgement' (MacDonald 1973, p. 83). It was not possible to define in advance what data would be significant, so that all data had initially to be accepted. 'In view of the potential significance of so many aspects of the project, a complete description of its experience was needed initially, as was awareness of a full range of relevant phenomena' (MacDonald 1973, p. 83). Selection within and between such data could only be made later when the criteria of such selection began to emerge from the continuing experience. 'Evaluation design, strategies and methods would evolve in response to the project's impact on the educational system and the types of evaluation problems which that impact would throw up' (MacDonald 1973, p. 83).

In this spirit the work of the 36 schools which experimented with the project was monitored, all possible techniques being used to collect a wide variety of data. Then attention was narrowed to eight schools which became the subjects of detailed case studies. The procedure appears to have been entirely justified since this method resulted in the acquisition of data and a recognition of phenomena that would never have been expected or envisaged in advance of the project's arrival in the classroom (MacDonald 1973).

Furthermore, there also emerged from this holistic approach a number of principles of wider significance for curriculum planning as a whole rather than merely for the evaluation of this particular project, principles which reflect in an interesting way some of the general points that have recently been made about curriculum development.

For example, it emerged very clearly that what actually happens when a project is put into practice varies considerably according to the local conditions prevailing in each school, whereas more simple evaluation procedures have tended to assume that there is or should be very little variation between schools. It also became apparent that curriculum innovations have many unexpected results and that again these are not allowed for in simple evaluation procedures. Furthermore, the variations in the reaction of different schools led to the conclusion that the judgements of the teachers in them are crucially important, every bit as important as those of the project designers, in the making of decisions concerning the curriculum of any individual school. It also became obvious that a gap often yawned between the conception of a project held by its developers and that held by those implementing it in the school. 'We have seen the Project used as a political resource in an existing power struggle, as a way of increasing the effectiveness of a custodial pattern of pupil control, and as a means of enhancing the image of institutions which covet the wrappings, but not the merchandise of innovation' (MacDonald 1971, p. 166; Stenhouse 1975, p. 111).

What was learnt from these processes of evaluation was seen, then, not as contributing to some statement of the project's effectiveness but as providing information for 'consumers', those who have the responsibility of making the decisions concerning the curriculum. Four main groups of these were identified — sponsors, local authorities, schools and examining boards — and the task of evaluation was seen as to provide them with the kind of understanding of the problems of curriculum development that will help them to make their decisions (MacDonald 1973).

The same general approach has been adopted by those who have proposed the notions of evaluation as 'portrayal' (Stake 1972) and as 'illumination' (Parlett and Hamilton 1976). Portrayal evaluation is seen as an attempt not to analyse the results of a project in terms of its pre-specified goals but to offer a comprehensive portrayal of the programme which will view it as a whole and endeavour to reveal its total substance.

Similarly, the primary concern of illuminative evaluation is 'with description and interpretation rather than measurement and prediction' (Parlett and Hamilton 1976, p. 88). Such an approach to evaluation has three stages — 'investigators observe, inquire further and then seek to explain' (Parlett and Hamilton 1976, p. 92). As a result of this three-fold procedure an 'information profile' is put together which is then available for those who need to make decisions about the project. 'Illuminative evaluation thus concentrates on the information-gathering rather than the decision-making component of evaluation. The task is to provide a comprehensive understanding of the complex reality (or realities) surrounding the project: in short, to "illuminate". In his report, therefore, the evaluator aims to sharpen discussion, disentangle complexities, isolate the significant from the trivial, and raise the level of sophistication of debate' (Parlett and Hamilton 1976, p. 99).

In similar style, the objectives of the evaluation unit of the Humanities Curriculum Project were defined as:

---

a) to ascertain the effects of the project, document the circumstances in which they occurred, and present this information in a form which would help educational decision-makers to evaluate the likely consequences of adopting the programme;

b) to describe the existing situation and operations of the schools being studied so that decision-makers could understand more fully what it was they were trying to change;

c) to describe the work of the project team in terms which would help the sponsors and planners of such ventures to weigh the value of this form of investment, and to determine more precisely the framework of support, guidance and control which were appropriate;

d) to make a contribution to evaluation theory by articulating problems clearly, recording experiences and, perhaps most important, publicising errors;

e) to contribute to the understanding of the problems of curriculum innovation generally.

(MacDonald 1973, p. 88.)

It is perhaps these last two points, and especially the last one of all, that are most interesting and draw our attention to the full significance of the developments in evaluation procedures consequent on the adoption of a non-objectives curriculum model. For what seems to be emerging as a result of the work of projects of this kind is a new and more sophisticated model of curriculum evaluation — a process model — which does not content itself with measuring the results of one project in simple and often consequentially unhelpful terms but sets out to provide continuous feedback to all of those concerned with the planning and implementation of this particular project and of curriculum development generally. Its concern is to disclose the meaning of the curriculum as much as to assess its worth (Stenhouse 1975). In some situations this will be done to help the planners to modify their objectives and other features of the project in the light of developing experience; in other circumstances it will be concerned to guide the continuing development of a non-objectives curriculum. Furthermore, the aim will be to do this not only in relation to one particular project but to offer illumination for curriculum development as a whole. The holistic approach to curriculum evaluation implies that we do not restrict ourselves to a narrow canvas.

Thus curriculum evaluation becomes part of curriculum research. In general, all evaluation procedures see all curriculum planning and approaches as hypotheses to be tested (Taba 1962), but the holistic view sees evaluation as part of a continuous programme of research and development, and recognizes that the curriculum is a dynamic and continuously evolving entity. It thus offers us a more sophisticated model not only of curriculum evaluation but also of curriculum planning and one which may be more suited to the notion of education as a process whose ends cannot be seen beyond itself.

Not only is it possible, then, to make an evaluation of a non-objectives curriculum; it also seems to lead to a more fully developed view of the role of evaluation in curriculum development. The procedural principles which we suggested in Chapter 2 provided a better basis for an educational activity than prespecified objectives can and should be monitored, and this monitoring will give us continuous feedback in our efforts constantly to modify and improve our practices. Again, as we saw in Chapter 2, such a model reflects much more accurately than a simple means/end model what happens in practice when we make an evaluation of any educational activity. For we are seldom content merely to measure outcomes and, when we do, we experience uneasy feelings that we have somehow missed the educational point of the activity. The simple linear model of curriculum evaluation, therefore, exists only at the conceptual level and is probably of little value even there.

One last point remains to be examined as a direct consequence of what we have just asserted about the possibility of evaluating a non-objectives curriculum. That is the question of whether it is acceptable to have a variety of models of curriculum evaluation. The issue is not so much whether we need to prestate our objectives in order to make evaluation possible but rather whether it is permissible to have different views of what evaluation is or whether all curriculum projects should be measured against a single yardstick or by a single scheme. It will be quite clear that a wide variety of evaluation procedures have emerged, for example, from the work of the many different Schools Council projects (Schools Council 1973). It is equally clear that to be effective and to provide the right kind of useful feedback data the procedures adopted must be closely related to the curriculum model that is being used. The question of whether it is acceptable to use different models of evaluation is therefore secondary to the question of whether it is possible to use different models of the curriculum itself. In discussing the question of curriculum objectives in Chapter 2, we suggested that it might be appropriate to approach both the planning and the execution of projects in different subject areas from appropriately different points of view. If this is so, then clearly these differences must extend into our evaluation procedures. However, this is an area that will obviously bear a good deal of further investigation.

This question of whether different models of evaluation are permissible leads to the related question of whether it is appropriate that different kinds of people should be involved in evaluating a curriculum. Who should have this task and responsibility? It is to this question that we must next turn.

The evaluator

The decision as to who should evaluate any particular curriculum innovation would seem *prima facie* to hinge on what are considered to be the main purposes of the evaluation process. If we are attempting to obtain data for administrative purposes then one kind of solution to the problem will seem appropriate; if, on the other hand, we are concerned to learn something about the problems of curriculum innovation itself as, for example, was the concern of those evaluating the Keele Integrated Studies Project (Shipman 1972), then another answer will be preferred; if we are intending to compare the effects of a project with those of other projects in the same field, a third scheme will be suitable, and so on.

However, our purposes are seldom as clear-cut as this would suggest and in most cases we will be looking to our evaluative procedures for answers to a number of different questions. Furthermore, difficulties must arise from the fact that different people will have different perceptions and conceptions of any project (Shipman 1972), so that each will emphasize different purposes, look for different kinds of data and make different interpretations of the evidence obtained. In short, we must face the fact that to achieve any kind of objective evaluation of a project will be far from straightforward, whatever the official view of its purposes is.

Clearly, objectivity in evaluation is highly desirable but there are many barriers to its achievement which we should be aware of. At one level, we would expect those people who have been closely involved in a project as administrators or planners or as teachers to have a commitment of some kind to it that is likely to make any kind of objective appraisal very difficult for them. However, as we have just suggested, the problem goes deeper than this, for all of those connected with a project will hold different definitions of it and different views of its nature. As a result, they will conceive the project differently, making different assumptions about its goals and purposes. They will also perceive things differently, since clearly our perceptions are affected by the values we hold; we see what we are looking for. Furthermore, the view an individual takes of the project will itself change continuously as his experience of the work grows.

Such differing views will be held even when the objectives of a project are clearly defined and stated, since there will be ample scope for individual preferences and rank orders within and between these objectives. The problem will be compounded, however, when we attempt to achieve objectivity in our evaluation of a non-objectives curriculum, when it is the intention that conceptions of the project and interpretations of it should change as the work develops.

What we are facing here in the context of curriculum evaluation is the more general problem we referred to briefly in Chapter 3 of whether objectivity is possible in any sphere, since the perceptions and interpretations of each individual are highly personal. Must we accept total subjectivity, as the phenomenologists suggest, or can we reach a definition of objectivity that is worthwhile?

Difficulties arise, as we saw in Chapter 3, when we see the search for objectivity as the pursuit of absolute certain knowledge of a God-given kind. Such knowledge we have already proposed is impossible in any sphere. We have suggested that a more realistic view of knowledge is that which sees it as a system of interrelated hypotheses, each of which fits the evidence we have but is also subject to amendment or rejection in the face of new evidence. What is essential is that we recognize the need for evidence, that this evidence should be public and that it should be considered with as much impartiality as is possible.

In short, it may be better to think not so much in terms of achieving objectivity in some absolute sense as of avoiding the most extreme forms of subjectivity that derive from views that are totally idiosyncratic or blindly prejudiced (Hamlyn 1972). This we can best do by recognizing the need to communicate our views, values and interpretations to others, to produce evidence in support of our claims and to be prepared to discuss them with others who may perceive or interpret things differently in as impartial and open a manner as we can achieve. Objectivity comes from recognizing the need to give reasons for our judgements and thus to open them up to rational discussion and debate.

Who should evaluate a curriculum project in order to achieve this kind of objectivity? Again *prima facie* it would seem that we might get closest to it by arranging for external evaluation. This is certainly the feeling of those who advocate the monitoring of standards of achievement in the centralized compulsory core of the curriculum by such people as local or government inspectors and it is also the principle that underlies systems of public examinations. How appropriate is it to the evaluation of a curriculum itself as opposed to the performance of individiual pupils engaged on it?

The main difficulty with such an approach to evaluation would seem to stem from the fact we have referred to on several occasions that all curriculum projects are highly complex entities with an intricate inter-linking of theoretical and practical elements of a kind that it is unlikely anyone could understand from the outside. External evaluation of this kind therefore would almost certainly lead to an oversimplification which would do violence to the project itself. It is unlikely, for example, that it could go much beyond the assessment of the levels of attainment of individual pupils and we have already referred to the lash-back effects of that on curriculum development through systems of public examinations.

To avoid this oversimplification and to achieve the breadth of understanding necessary to make a useful evaluation of the wider aspects of a project, such an outside person would need to get inside the project, to become a specialist evaluator. It is for this reason that in most cases evaluators have been appointed as members of project teams. The point at which the evaluator joins the team varies. In some cases, as with the Science 5-13 Project, he or she has been appointed at the beginning to be involved from the outset in the framing of objectives, purposes or principles (Tawney 1973). In other cases, such as the Cambridge School Classics Project, the evaluator has joined the team at a later stage when much of the groundwork has been completed (Tawney 1973). Whatever the relative merits of these alternatives, they both recognize the need for the evaluator to become involved in the overall planning in order that he should be able to achieve an understanding of the complexities of the project, whether his job is merely to assess its outcomes or to contribute through his skills as an evaluator to the ongoing development of the scheme. In other words, whatever view is taken of the purposes of evaluation and whatever model is adopted, it is recognized that it is desirable and necessary for the evaluator to join the project team at some stage in order to become in a full sense a part of the project.

We must finally consider the role of the teacher in curriculum evaluation. There is little doubt that the teacher is the person who possesses a good deal of the data the evaluator needs so that he or she must be seen as having an important contribution to make to evaluation at that level. Thus, for example, one of the techniques used in the evaluation of the Schools Council's Social Education Project was the recording of interviews with teachers who had worked with the programme. In this way, the teachers' views were canvassed on a range of issues:

1) What do you think of the Social Education Project as it affects the pupils?

2) Do you think they have been given too much or too little responsibility?

3) Has it had any effect on the community round about?

4) What has been the effect of the project on the staff of the school as a whole?

5)   How much of the work is new?

6)   How would you like the work to develop?

7)   Should there be more opportunities for exchange of experiences with teachers in other schools engaged in similar work?

8)   Has there been enough discussion and planning among teachers concerned within your own school?

9)   How can the work be evaluated?

10)   Is there anything you would like to add?

(Schools Council 1974a, pp. 52-53.)

In this way it was hoped that the experience of the teachers could be tapped to provide crucial data for evaluation.

In connection with this kind of process, Wynne Harlen makes an interesting additional point, that any techniques of evaluation that one uses should 'interfere as little as possible with . . . the activities which are going on', and should not be 'arduous or laborious for either children or teachers. It is most important that the evaluation does not interfere, does not reduce enthusiasm, is as unobtrusive as possible and, where it has to be obtrusive, at least enjoyable' (Harlen 1971, p. 132).

However, many have seen the role of the teacher in evaluation as going beyond being a mere provider of data. Again Wynne Harlen has summed this up in saying that 'teachers should be as thoroughly and genuinely involved in the evaluation as they are, or should be, with the development of the material' (Harlen 1971, p. 133). They should not merely be asked to provide data, especially where this is mainly a form-filling exercise, but should be involved in continuous discussion of the questions being asked. The effects of this are two-way. For in the first place the teachers develop the kind of understanding of the problems of evaluation that will make them better at providing appropriate data and, secondly, the evaluators can gain insights that will lead to a better framing of questions. Teachers can and should also be involved in the testing and marking of children where this is included in the evaluation process. Full involvement of teachers in all aspects of the development of a curriculum project is crucial to maximizing its success. 'Improved attitudes of teachers towards evaluation will certainly follow from improved attitudes of evaluators towards teachers' (Harlen 1971, p. 133).

Serious barriers do exist, however, to the achievement by teachers of anything approaching an objective appraisal of what after all they are responsible for at the coal face as some of the work of the Ford Teaching Project has revealed. A key concern of this project was to get teachers to evaluate their own work, to engage in a kind of self-monitoring process and it was assumed that this implied the adoption by the teacher of an objective stance. It is not easy for teachers, however, as those concerned with the project discovered, to create a situation in which pupils can with confidence tell them what they really think about a particular piece of work. The whole idea of self-criticism and self-monitoring is threatening to many teachers; the organizational set-up in most schools does not help teachers to engage in this kind of self-appraisal; and many teachers find it difficult to discuss their problems with their colleagues (Elliott and Adelman 1974).

The experience of those engaged in the Ford Teaching Project, however, led them to be 'optimistic about the capacity of the majority of teachers for self-criticism' (Elliott and Adelman 1974, p. 23) and to assume that the barriers to objectivity in such cases are no more than practical difficulties which can be overcome. They also realized that subjectivity of evaluation can in any case be avoided by checking the accounts teachers give of their work by reference to other sources. Thus they developed a procedure they called multiple interview or triangulation in which accounts are obtained not only from the teacher but also from the pupils and an independent observer. There is reason to hope, therefore, that given the right sort of training, preparation and adequate safeguards, teachers should be able to play an increasingly important role in curriculum evaluation.

Furthermore, it has been suggested that objective methods of assessment are in any case not always appropriate and that in certain areas the subjective assessment of teachers might be what is needed, especially in the affective domain. Thus the Schools Council's exploration of 'Education through the use of materials', to which we have already referred, suggests that in assessing certain objectives in the affective domain 'the subjective assessment of the teacher may be of value, and if it is conducted within a clearly defined structure it may give a useful appraisal of the attainment of pupils in terms of specified educational objectives' (Schools Council 1969a, p. 11). It goes on to say, 'More objective measurement may be applied to the assessment of the attainment of other objectives, but it must be recognized that objective methods may not be appropriate for measuring the effectiveness of all existing or new teaching methods' (Schools Council 1969a, p. 11).

In general, however, it does appear that evaluation, like curriculum development itself, is best attained when a variety of talents and points of view are brought to bear on it. Certainly one of the best ways to avoid the worst kind of subjectivity is to encourage a number of people to contribute to the evaluation processes from different points of view. It is probably the case that for a complex undertaking of this kind a skilled specialist evaluator is necessary, but it is equally necessary that all who are involved in the planning and execution of it, including the pupils, should be seen as having a point of view and, therefore, a contribution to make towards its evaluation. That contribution must go beyond merely providing data for the evaluator; it must entail full partnership in the process of evaluation itself.

This is another dimension of the holistic approach to evaluation that we have already discussed. Not only are all kinds of data grist to the evaluator's mill, but also all those involved in the process are to be seen as evaluators. We saw earlier that a holistic approach sees evaluation as an integral part of curriculum development; it represents a form of continuous action-research and feedback. If this is so and if the desirability of school-based curriculum development is recognized, there is an important role for the teacher in curriculum evaluation as much as in any other aspect of curriculum development. For who needs this continuous feedback more than he does? Without it self-evaluation will be impossible and thus so will any real progress for the teacher and the project. This points us towards the notion of 'democratic' evaluation, as opposed to 'autocratic' or 'bureaucratic' evaluation, of which 'the basic value is an informed citizenry, and the evaluator acts as a broker in exchanges of information between groups who want knowledge of each other' (MacDonald 1975, p. 134; Stenhouse 1975, p. 121).

'Democratic' evaluation is that style of evaluation that is designed to inform the teacher and others and to help forward curriculum development, whereas both the 'bureaucratic' and 'autocratic' styles are concerned with forms of external validation in accordance with the values of those who either control the purse strings or conduct from without the process of evaluation. This is a distinction we must take up again in our discussion of a common curriculum in Chapter 7.

Lawrence Stenhouse, while largely approving of the general trend of such a development towards a 'democratic' style of evaluation, is concerned about the emergence of the professional evaluator as well as of the professional curriculum developer or at least about the separation of these two roles. He is concerned to promote integrated curriculum research and sees this kind of development as inimical to it. 'Evaluation should, as it were, lead development and be integrated with it. Then the conceptual distinction between development and evaluation is destroyed and the two merge as research' (Stenhouse 1975, p. 122).

The force of this case must be recognized, but two points need to be made in answer to it. In the first place, evaluation must provide continuous feedback into the development of the total curriculum and not only into the work of a particular project (Wilhelms 1971), a point which we saw above was one of Barry MacDonald's stated objectives of evaluation. For this reason it must be in the hands of a team that will include others besides the teachers and project planners or designers concerned with a particular project. What is required is essentially a team effort involving cooperation at all stages (Taba 1962). Secondly, a proper evaluation, particularly if it is to be an integral part of curriculum development in this way, will also require the use of many different techniques of evaluation and the use of these is essentially a job for a specialist or a team of specialists. There are limits to the list of duties one can reasonably expect the teacher to take on.

It is necessary, however, to recognize a problem and perhaps a danger here. For in such a cooperative venture the teacher is likely always to be dependent on those who come from outside, since by definition they are bringing something into the situation that he cannot supply (Elliott and Adelman 1973). Thus the teacher's autonomy is at risk.

On the other hand, the question of teacher-accountability is also raised and this perhaps provides another reason why evaluation should be undertaken by a team that includes outsiders. There seems to be a central role for the teacher in the evaluation of the curriculum as part of curriculum planning and development generally, but what that role is has not yet become clear. This is a point we must take up again, therefore, in the final chapters.

In the meantime, one thing at least is clear, and that is that most teachers do not possess at present the necessary understanding of the techniques that have been used in evaluation.

It is only comparatively recently that the complexities of evaluation processes have come to be recognized and as a result the need for a complex range of evaluation techniques. It is not long since the only technique used was the assessment of the progress of individual pupils so that evaluation was regarded as synonymous with assessment and even with examinations. Thus a good many books that purported to discuss evaluation offered little more than an analysis of assessment techniques.

Two things have happened to change this. In the first place, it has been realized that learning is a highly complex thing and that we need a range of sophisticated techniques to measure it properly. Secondly, the complexities of curriculum development and evaluation in themselves have come to be recognized, as we have just seen, so that an awareness has grown that in order to begin to come close to an adequate form of evaluation procedure one must use a variety of techniques to collect relevant data across a wide spectrum.

Unfortunately, although the scope of education has changed and expanded rapidly in recent years, the development of techniques of evaluation has not really proceeded at the same pace. More recently, however, the growing awareness of the need to collect all kinds of data in order to evaluate a curriculum has led to the use of a wider variety of techniques, some of which we have referred to already in other contexts. These include assessments made by independent evaluators and the gathering of evidence of all kinds from teachers, pupils and any other people involved in the work. Thus the Schools Council's Social Education Project, to which we have already referred, lists among the techniques adopted and developed for part of its evaluation processes:

1)   teacher interviews;

2)   a list of pupils' responses to the concept of social education;

3)   interviews with a small but random sample of parents;

4)   a test of attitudes to school especially developed for the project;

5)   a test of children's accuracy in self-perception and peer-perception;

6)   evaluation of constructiveness of contributions to group discussion

(Schools Council 1974a, p. 51).

It is clear from this that progress is being made towards the generation of more sophisticated techniques of evaluation to measure the more complex dimensions of recent curriculum development. It will also be clear, perhaps, that the more sophisticated these techniques become the more necessary it will be for the teacher to have the aid of specialists in these techniques in evaluating the curriculum and basing decisions about future changes and innovations on the data they produce.

It is equally apparent, however, that the main focus of evaluation continues to be on the progress of the individual pupil, whether this be defined in terms of his increased knowledge and understanding or, as in the example given, in terms of the development of attitudes or skills of a different kind. The implications for curriculum development of systems of public examinations for the assessment of the progress of individual pupils we must take up in the next chapter where we shall consider several such external influences on curriculum development.

Summary and conclusions

This chapter has tried to examine some of the problems of curriculum evaluation and to suggest ways in which evaluation techniques can be used not only to avoid the worst kinds of inhibiting backlash on curriculum planning but actually to promote and contribute to its continuing development. We have argued that this can only be achieved by a 'democratic' form of evaluation in which teachers themselves are involved, so that they can both gain the understanding and enjoy the freedom necessary to the making of wise decisions about the curriculum. Finally, we suggested that they would need to be assisted in this by specialist evaluators who could develop advanced techniques to obtain the data necessary for decisions of this kind.

Several things have emerged as by-products, as it were, of our discussion of evaluation. One of these is the clear need for accountability. A second and related issue is the need to get the right balance between the role of the teacher and that of various outside agencies, both those concerned to disseminate curriculum innovations and those that influence curriculum change in more subtle ways or attempt to keep a check on the general trends of curriculum development.

We must now turn to a consideration of these forces and the inter-relationships between them — the strategies and realities of curriculum change — as a further aspect of our examination of the theory and the practice of curriculum development.

CHAPTER 6

THE SOCIAL CONTEXT OF CURRICULUM DEVELOPMENT

Up to this point we have discussed curriculum development as though it goes on in a world populated only by teachers and other educationists. We have looked at many of the theoretical and practical difficulties of curriculum planning and the implementation of curriculum innovation, at the theoretical questions that lie behind curriculum planning and some of their practical consequences, as if the intentions of teachers and other curriculum developers were the only factors we need to take account of, as if they were entirely and solely in control of curriculum change.

Our discussion so far, then, has proceeded on the basis of two unwarranted assumptions. The first of these is that influences outside education are not important in affecting what is taught in schools and that curriculum development is entirely a matter of careful planning on the part of the professionals. Secondly, we have assumed that, so long as we take full account of the practical implications of the plans we make for the curriculum, as was suggested in Denis Lawton's model of curriculum planning which we mentioned in Chapter 1, there will be no significant gap between the theory and the practice of curriculum development, between the designing of curriculum programmes and their realization in practice. With these assumptions we have looked at several models of curriculum planning and we have considered some of the theoretical and practical difficulties that arise over the framing of objectives, the choosing of appropriate content and the setting up of adequate procedures of evaluation.

We suggested in Chapter 1, however, that this was only one aspect of curriculum change and development and that there were many other factors at work that we must take full cognisance of. We have also hinted throughout that there is a very wide gap between what is planned and what actually happens, between the official and the actual curriculum, between the ideals and conceptions in the minds of the curriculum planners and the realities of the outcomes of these in the classroom.

We must now, therefore, give due consideration to these two important aspects of curriculum change by looking at the other pressures that are at work, the other influences both direct and indirect, overt and covert, deliberate and incidental, that play their part in curriculum change and development. We must also consider the crucial question of how, in the face of these many, and often conflicting, pressures, curriculum change actually comes about, how the planning achieves realization and how as a result it can best be promoted.

This we will do by considering first of all the influences of the public examination and some of the other influences and constraints that act upon curriculum planning, some factors other than the ideas of educationists which either promote or inhibit curriculum change. We will then consider the problems these factors create for the dissemination of curriculum innovation and the resultant gap that can often be discerned between the theory and the practice of curriculum development. This will lead us inevitably to examine in more detail the role of the teacher in curriculum development and the related issues of how far such development should or can take place at the level of the individual school and how such a process of school-based curriculum development might be supported. These are largely uncharted waters but, since it is beginning to appear that we shall need to navigate them in our search for the right form of curriculum development, some exploration of what they might hold is vital. Finally, if we are to consider the possibility of placing a high responsibility for curriculum development in the hands of individual schools and groups of teachers, we must consider the question of the control of the curriculum and how far it should be in the hands of the teachers themselves, a question that will lead us naturally to our discussion of the notion of a centralized curriculum in the final chapter.

Public examinations and curriculum development

We have already suggested on several occasions that the limitations of the techniques available for evaluation may lead to limitations in the educational goals that teachers set for themselves and their pupils, that the temptation always exists to plan our curriculum according to the techniques of evaluation that are available. It is clear that this is most likely to occur in relation to the assessment of the progress of individual pupils. Indeed, we have already also referred several times to the degree to which many teachers regard the public examination system as the chief inhibitor of curriculum change and support for this view can be found in the obvious back-lash effects that the 11+ system of selection for secondary education had on the curriculum of the primary school.

We also suggested in the last chapter that the assessment of individual pupils remains the major source of data for evaluation, so that, while this continues to be so, the assessment techniques available to us will continue to be a major potential source of limitations on curriculum development. We must begin this discussion of the external influences on the curriculum, therefore, with a brief consideration of the examining techniques that are available for use and some attempt to indicate ways in which this kind of assessment may be undertaken without unduly inhibiting curriculum development.

It is not the intention here to raise the interesting questions of how far and in what ways the assessment of individual pupils provides adequate data for evaluating the curriculum itself. Nor is it the intention to look in detail at the present structure of the public examination system in the United Kingdom or elsewhere or to examine the many proposals that are currently under discussion for substantial changes in that structure, fascinating though such a discussion might be. These we will refer to only in so far as they impinge upon or have relevance for our central concern.

That concern will be with the effects of systems of public examinations on curriculum development and the question of whether such effects need to be inhibiting. In other words, it will be the intention to consider the claim that curriculum development is inhibited by public examination systems, to try to tease out what factors might be responsible for this and to explore ways in which the worst of these effects might be avoided, ways in which the system might be modified or features of the system that might be promoted in order to resolve some of the problems it creates for teachers and others concerned with curriculum development.

We should perhaps begin by making it clear that what is needed is to find some way in which continuous curriculum development and the demands of the public examination can be reconciled. It is clearly not acceptable, as some extremists seem to think, to abolish examination systems totally in order to free the curriculum from their pressures. What is needed is to devise an acceptable working relationship between the two. For public examination systems serve several essential purposes. Amongst other things and apart from the data they may provide for evaluating the curriculum, they contribute more than any other agency to the setting and maintaining of educational and academic standards; they provide incentives to the efforts of both teachers and pupils; they provide useful diagnostic feedback for both; and they fulfil an important administrative function in revealing the talents and abilities of individuals and indicating their suitability for certain kinds of career or further educational experiences. The fact that a high degree of inefficiency becomes apparent when one considers the extent to which current procedures do fulfil these administrative functions, of which the manifest errors of the 11+ (Yates and Pidgeon 1975) and the lack of predictive validity of current GCE 'A' level examinations in relation to subsequent achievements in higher education are perhaps the best available examples, should encourage us to look in more detail at the procedures themselves rather than to assume that the only solution is to scrap them altogether.

What is needed is a close consideration of public examination systems to ensure that they both provide those who need it with the right kind of accurate information about the achievements and perhaps also the potential of individual pupils and that they do this without placing undue limitations on curriculum development.

Both of these aspects of the problem require that we consider the public examination from two points of view, first of all from the point of view of the techniques of assessment available to those conducting the examination and, secondly, from the point of view of the way in which the examination procedures are structured and the system organized and administered. For both of these dimensions of the system have been criticized as resulting in the production of the wrong kind of information about pupils while at the same time inhibiting curriculum change in the schools.

It is often claimed that the techniques of assessment available to examiners are so relatively unsophisticated that they cannot properly measure any but the most simple of educational objectives and that as a result they lead both to the production of unhelpful information for 'consumers' and to the generation of simple curricula by teachers. The word most commonly used in association with the public examination is 'regurgitation' and the criticism is that the ability to regurgitate largely undigested material (a rather revolting but popular metaphor) is all that most examinations demand, so that their results indicate merely the degree to which pupils can do this — information which is not really very helpful to a potential employer or an institution of further or higher education. Also, this general feature of public examinations invites teachers to aim no higher in their courses than to get pupils to swallow large quantities of information in preparation for regurgitating it at the appropriate time and place. There is the further inference, if we can take this unpleasant metaphor to its equally unpleasant conclusion, that once this material has been regurgitated, then, like the contents of an undigested and regurgitated meal, it is gone for ever. Furthermore, the same is usually true of all taste and liking for that particular kind of sustenance. In this way, it is argued, the examination system inhibits not only curriculum development but the development of anything that could be described as education.

At a deeper level, what is being argued is that the examination system cannot cope with more complex educational objectives, a point that we considered earlier in relation to evaluation procedures generally. Within the cognitive domain, for example, it is sometimes felt that it cannot measure the higher kinds of cognitive achievement, such as understanding and application, and thus contents itself with the lower levels, such as memorization and rote learning. If this is so, then it must follow that within the affective domain it hardly begins at all, so that teachers may be wasting their own and their pupils time — in terms of examination results — if they devote too much attention to developing attitudes and feelings in their students towards the subject or material they are dealing with. The methods of assessment will thus decide the nature of the curriculum and how teachers and pupils view it and receive it (Wilhelms 1971).

This may be a caricature of the public examination system but, like all caricatures, it does emphasize a salient feature of its subject and we cannot dismiss this charge with too ready a complacency. Most of those who read this book will have reached a high level in the education system; few will have done so without achieving some of their 'qualifications' by methods not dissimilar to those we have just described. That such things happen is indisputable.

The real question, however, is whether this is how things must be. Can these effects be avoided? There is reason to believe that they can and recent developments in examination procedures tend to encourage such a view. For the range of techniques used in assessment is gradually being extended and the manner in which each is used is becoming more sophisticated.

In addition to the written essay-type examination paper, which traditionally has been the most common device for assessing pupils' progress, recent years have seen the arrival or increased use of such techniques as 'open-book' examinations, prior disclosure techniques, the objective test, oral examinations, practical tests, continuous assessment through the examination of course work of many kinds and the use of teacher-assessments. This range of techniques increases enormously the scope of assessment procedures to measure a wide variety of achievements in both the cognitive and the affective domains, if we can make best use of it. It also increases the possibility of our being able to obtain accurate and useful data both about the curriculum itself and the performance of individual pupils.

It has also been realized that each of these techniques can be used more subtly to obtain more complex information. The essay-type written examination can test more than factual knowledge and memorization if we frame our questions suitably and even the objective test, whose *prima facie* role would seem to be to test factual knowledge, has been shown to be capable of measuring higher level cognitive attainments too (Vernon 1964). For example, knowledge that goes beyond the mere factual can be measured, as in questions such as the following:

In the view of John Ruskin, the greatest picture is:

a) that which imitates best

b) that which teaches us most.

c) that which exhibits the greatest power.

d) that which conveys the greatest number of the greatest ideas.

(Vernon 1964, p. 8.)

So too can comprehension be measured in an objective test, as in:

'Milton! thou shouldst be living at this hour: England hath need of thee; she is a fen of stagnant waters' — Wordsworth. The metaphor, 'she is a fen of stagnant waters', indicates that Wordsworth felt that England was,

a) largely swampy land.

b) in a state of turmoil and unrest.

c) making no progress.

d) in a generally corrupt condition.

(Vernon 1964, p. 8.)

Furthermore, similar questions can be devised to measure such higher level cognitive skills as application, analysis, synthesis and evaluation.

It would seem inappropriate, therefore, to assume that the examination system need tempt us into settling for simple objectives to our teaching. Both the range of techniques available and the uses that can be made of each of them offer scope for the development of more subtle instruments of examining than were once available to us.

Suspicion of the newer techniques still exists, however, at all levels of education. Teachers like to hold on to their myths as much as any body of people and the view that the written examination paper is the only source of really objective information about pupils dies very hard. Thus other techniques have been slow to achieve acceptance especially in the more prestigious examinations. In the United Kingdom, for example, the use of course-work assessment procedures was built into the regulations governing the award of the Certificate of Secondary Education (CSE) examinations from their inception but has been very slow to achieve acceptance by the more prestigious and, perhaps, status-conscious General Certificate of Education (GCE) Boards. Indeed, the strange truth is that it has been accepted by the universities themselves for use in their own degree examinations more readily than by the schools examination boards they sponsor.

One reason for this is clearly a real concern people have about the possibilities of plagiarism and other forms of dishonesty in the production of work that is not written under complete supervision. The dangers of this should not be underestimated, although they are not insuperable and should not deter us from adopting a technique that has other manifest advantages.

The objections of some, however, go beyond this, since there are real doubts in the minds of some teachers and educationists about the validity of some of these new and alternative techniques of assessment. As a result, there is a reluctance to adopt some of these techniques because of a concern about their relative validity. It is interesting to note, therefore, that there is some evidence which suggests that the concurrent validity of some of these techniques, especially course-work assessment, is high (Connaughton 1969). In other words, in comparison with other methods of assessment used simultaneously, these techniques appear far more accurate than their critics seem to think.

There is reason to hope, therefore, that the development of increasingly sophisticated techniques for the assessment of pupils' progress, a development which recent years have seen make considerable advances, can result in our being able to establish procedures for public examinations which need not limit our curricular ambitions and may at the same time provide potential employers and teachers in further and higher educational institutions with information about individuals more suited to their needs. What is needed is that we recognize the different functions of these techniques and develop the right combinations of them to provide us with the information we need and to measure all relevant aspects of the activities in which we engage our pupils. One simple truth to cling to is that it is unlikely that the use of only one kind of assessment technique can measure all that we should be concerned with in any educational activity. The use of combinations of techniques, on the other hand, ought to increase quite extensively our scope for the development of the kind of educational curricula we want.

There remains, however, the problem of ensuring that the curriculum can develop continuously. This brings us naturally, therefore, to our second main point — the organization of the public examination systems themselves and especially the role of the individual teacher within them. It is one thing to say that, however complex our curriculum is, the examination system can assess the progress of pupils within it; it is quite another to devise a system that allows not only for the generation of a complex curriculum but also for its continuing evolution and development. It is this feature of the examination system that has led many teachers to feel that it gives them no scope for change or development or the exercise of individual professional autonomy, even though it does seem essential that the examination system should reflect and follow from the curriculum rather than directing and leading curriculum development.

The first aspect of this problem is the development of examinations for new subjects or areas that are introduced into the curriculum. It will be clear that no curriculum innovation will get beyond the third year of the secondary school or will be made accessible to the more able pupils unless its development is accompanied by the establishment of an accepted public examination.

It is for this reason that most of the curriculum projects designed for use in secondary schools by the Schools Council have been aimed at pupils of average and below average ability. For their planners have been aware that the demands of the examination system would make it unlikely that schools would be able or willing to adopt new schemes for use with their abler pupils. Thus many curriculum innovations, such as the Humanities Curriculum Project, have more often than not been made available only to those of average and below average ability and in this way the more able pupils have been deprived of important experiences and debarred from areas of learning or exploration that would seem to have as much value for them as for any other pupils. It is surely not the case, for example, that you do not need a moral or a social education if you can gain seven or eight 'O' level passes in academic subjects.

It is also clear that the existence of public examinations in a subject raises the status of that subject in the eyes of both pupils and parents. Those concerned with a subject like rural studies, for example, while worried about the possibly inhibiting effects of examinations on sylla-buses, nevertheless recognize that their subject 'suffers because it does not possess the hallmark stamped upon the older disciplines by the provision of 'A' and 'O' level examinations' (Schools Council 1969b, p. 22), and that where examinations have been introduced these 'have helped to improve the image of the subject and to give it a certain status in the eyes of the pupils and their parents' (Schools Council 1969b, p. 12).

Establishing such new examinations is not an easy process but that it can be done has been demonstrated by the use made by individual schools and others of the facilities that exist within the CSE regulations and those of some GCE boards such as the Associated Examining Board (AEB) for the approval and assessment of school-based projects (Kelly 1974a; Smith and Macintosh 1974; Kelly 1975). If schools are to be able to introduce new areas of study into their curricula they must have procedures for ensuring that the work of the pupils in these areas can be assessed.

The second problem is to ensure continuous development within subject areas. This is perhaps the point at which teachers feel that the public examinations' shoe pinches most. Even if they feel they have good reasons for modifying what they are doing, they will not act on these unless they can be sure that the modifications they make will be reflected in the examinations their pupils are set. Without this they will feel that they are putting their pupils at risk by altering their approach or the content of their teaching. How can these constraints be avoided or minimized without our going to the other extreme of removing external evaluation and checks from the curriculum altogether?

One possible solution to this problem lies in a greater involvement of those responsible for the external examinations in curriculum development itself (Macintosh 1970). That the examining board can use its power not only to inhibit but to promote and direct curriculum development is clear from those instances where this has been done. A look at the history of public examinations in the United Kingdom will reveal the extent to which the procedures of the examination system have influenced the development of the curriculum. The change from a School Certificate requiring evidence of simultaneous achievement in a wide range of subjects to the GCE which can be achieved in one subject only or in a series of subjects examined at different times had a major influence on the development of the curriculum of the secondary schools. It was even claimed in 1971 that 'within the context of any given single subject, CSE and some GCE examinations had brought in new ideas and syllabuses which were an improvement on previous practice' (Schools Council 1971c, p. 16). An example of this to which we have already referred is the major changes brought about in the teaching of handicraft, in fact in its total conversion to design and technology, by the University of London GCE Board of Examiners in the subject (Hicks 1974). This is one extreme way in which an examining board can involve itself in curriculum development.

It should be equally possible, however, for a board to take a less directive role in the development of a curriculum while being effectively involved in the generation of objectives and decisions about suitable content and procedures. Unless such involvement can be achieved it will be difficult for others to go very far in effecting significant changes in the curriculum. Examination boards must then be given a new and participatory role in curriculum planning.

One way forward has been indicated by the collaboration that there has been between individual schools and examining boards in those examinations where, as in Mode 3 of the CSE, the development of school-based schemes has been permitted (Macintosh 1970). Quite often these schemes have entailed the use of continuous or course-work assessment techniques and these have the effect of involving teachers themselves in the assessment procedures or at least making it essential that they be involved in discussion with the examiners. The same is also true even where no more than a school-based written paper is to be set.

The possibilities of school-based examinations which can be standardized nationally have been well explored by their use within the CSE and the extension of this facility to all GCE examinations must surely not be far away. This is one way in which the inhibiting effects of the external examination on the curriculum can be minimized. It is clearly especially valuable if we wish our curriculum to be free from the need to begin from a clear specification of its objectives or intended outcomes and if we wish to allow for the fact that in some areas the most significant outcomes are those that defy clear definition in advance (Macintosh 1970).

What is crucial here, however, is not merely that the examination is school-based; it is that, being school-based, it is firmly in the control of the teachers or at least susceptible to their influence. It is often claimed that the public examination system has always been mainly in the hands of teachers. In one sense this is clearly true, since most examination boards have more members drawn from the ranks of teachers than from any other single source. To say that this gives adequate teacher participation in the assessment procedures, however, is to miss the real point. For these teachers will represent only a small proportion of those whose work is affected by the form of the examination and the others will be almost as effectively limited in their work as if all of the examiners came from outer space. What is needed is not that a few representative teachers should be involved in the setting and marking of examinations, but that all teachers who are involved in the development of the teaching of a subject should be involved in or have access to and influence on the actual assessment process (Macintosh 1970).

Safeguards against subjectivity of assessment, halo-effects and the like must, of course, be built into such procedures. That they can be is demonstrated by the experience of those boards which have experimented with school-based examinations and course-work assessment techniques and, indeed, by the well-established procedures of our universities which always examine their own students but at the same time employ external examiners from other universities to advise them, to monitor standards and to ensure as much objectivity as is possible. Similar inter-school and even extra-school moderation can be provided without depriving the teachers themselves of their central role in the assessment of their pupils. Unless they are given that central role, the public examination will continue to be the most effective inhibitor of curriculum development rather than being seen as one aspect of a total programme and itself subject to development in phase with the curriculum it is there to assess.

External examinations, however, are not the only source of constraints on teachers, nor are they the only factors that limit the freedom of teachers and head teachers to develop their work in whatever ways they wish. We must now, therefore, turn to a consideration of some of the other influences and constraints that play their part in curriculum development.

Influences and constraints

Even in a country such as the United Kingdom, where legal constraints on the curriculum are almost non-existent, it is far from being the case that the control of the curriculum is the sole prerogative of head teachers. For, although the legal responsibility rests with the head teacher of each school, he or she can only exercise the freedom that that responsibility offers within a context of countless pressures, influences and constraints from both within and without the school, so that the most interesting feature of school curricula in the United Kingdom is that, despite the apparent freedom enjoyed by individual schools, they vary extremely little, a fact which makes the demands for more centralized control over the curriculum, at least when couched in terms of content, appear rather superfluous. It would be difficult to find a school whose curriculum did not include most or all of what might be agreed as constituting such a central or essential core. In short, the head teacher, like all others, defines his role in relation to the expectations of other people who have significance for him.

We must now consider in detail some of the influences and constraints that affect decisions about the school curriculum.

We must first note the influence of history or tradition that we commented on in Chapter 1. Curriculm development is essentially a matter of changing a curriculum that already exists, and the demands of any entity to be left substantially untouched are always strong. Curriculum change is one aspect of social change so that it shares that tendency of all institutions to resist any attempts to do more than chip away at it and introduce relatively minor modifications.

In the case of curriculum change the reasons for this are not hard to find. Teachers and head teachers have been trained in certain ways, to teach certain subjects or by certain methods, so that there is a strong temptation for them not to want these changed to a degree which will require them to start again from scratch, to learn new techniques or to lose the security of working within a subject or a set of techniques with which they are at home and in which they are confident of their knowledge and ability. The same is true of those who leave the classroom and the school to join the ranks of the inspectorate or other advisory bodies. Too much change in the curriculum or in approaches to teaching and they will know less about what is going on and have less relevant experience than those they are supposed to inspect or advise.

This is one factor in the recent changes that have occurred in the role of the inspectorate and it is well illustrated by the plight of many inspectors and advisers in the face of the recent rapid move in many secondary schools in the United Kingdom towards mixed ability groupings. This is also one reason why the emphasis in initial training courses for teachers has swung away from mere training towards education, towards developing the kind of professional awareness and understanding that will enable teachers to initiate and adapt to changes. It is also a feature of the current educational scene which makes it imperative that adequate provision be made for the continuing education and training of teachers through in-service courses of all kinds. Tradition, then, does exercise a great constraining influence on curriculum development.

There are a number of different ways in which one can categorize the other influences and constraints to which curriculum development is subject. All of these do, of course, interact with each other but sometimes they also conflict, since often they emanate from groups of people and bodies who view the schools and the curriculum from different perspectives, as parents, for example, or as employers, as teachers or as economists. Some of the confusion that can be discerned in debate about the curriculum, as in the current national debate in the United Kingdom about the common core curriculum, derives from the fact that the several contributors to such debate are approaching it from different standpoints (Warwick 1975). If we are to avoid such confusion ourselves, we must, therefore, distinguish these standpoints at the outset.

To begin with it is worth distinguishing administrative from professional factors (Maclure 1970). Both of these will be sources of influences and constraints on developments in schools and they are also likely to be in conflict with each other more often than not. In particular, financial restrictions will invariably constrain and inhibit professional ambitions for certain kinds of development, such as a reduction in the size of class, improved in-service provision or any other contribution to curriculum development that involves increased financial support. Equally, however, decisions made about the organization of schooling, such as the introduction of comprehensive schools or the raising of the school-leaving age, may conflict with, although they may also on occasion support, certain professional aspirations for curriculum development. It has been suggested that this very conflict of forces provides the right kind of basis for change, since it allows for the interaction of and the development of a balance between these two major influences acting on education and curriculum change (Maclure 1970). It is for this reason that both of these interests are represented on such formal agencies for curriculum change as the Schools Council.

We must also distinguish national from local influences and within the latter those that operate inside the school from those outside it. It may also be important to differentiate between the role of the teacher in curriculum development and that of the head teacher and to recognize that different factors will operate or at least the same factors will operate with different degrees of impact on each. It is this that will result in the gap between the official and the actual curriculum, the ideal and the real, the formal and the operational that we have already referred to several times.

Lastly, it is also likely to be the case that the factors we can identify will be differentially significant at different levels of schooling. The factors that are most influential at primary level are unlikely to be those that have the greatest effect on the curriculum of the secondary school. It is almost certainly the case, for example, that national factors are most in evidence at secondary level while the primary school is more susceptible to local influences.

In all of these cases too, we must remember that these influences are likely at many points to be in conflict with each other, to be pulling in different directions, so that the kind of curriculum change that actually occurs will be the result of these many competing and conflicting forces.

The influence exercised by central government on curriculum development is obviously much greater in those countries where, or at those times in history when, formal decisions about the curriculum are taken centrally or where and when adherence to strict standards is made a requirement for grant-aid. Such influence is also very direct. In the United Kingdom this influence has gradually been eroded to the point where even Her Majesty's Inspectors play a relatively minor part in the development of the curriculum and the monitoring of standards and no direct control is exercised over the curriculum. A reaction against this has recently become apparent, however, and the creation by the Department of Education and Science of an Assessment of Performance Unit is one step towards the re-establishment of central control of this kind.

Even where such control is not direct, however, decisions about the organization of the educational system taken centrally will have implications for the curriculum. Again the most obvious example of this is the requirement of the British Government, made known in 1965, that all secondary education in the United Kingdom be organized on comprehensive lines. Such a decision cannot be implemented without far-reaching effects on curriculum development. Nor can a decision such as that to raise the minimum school-leaving age.

This draws our attention to other political influences on the curriculum of a more general kind. In those countries where there is a strong dominant political ideology, as is the case in most Communist countries, for example, that ideology will be reflected massively in the curriculum. In all countries, however, education is in the centre of the political arena, as will be apparent from the most cursory study of the development of education in the United Kingdom during the last fifty years or so. Furthermore, there are political pressure groups other than those associated with national political parties which are formed in order to promote certain kinds of educational reform or to influence educational development generally. Obvious among these are the teachers' unions and professional associations, but there are also bodies such as ACE, CASE and PRISE which have come into being as a result of the desire of groups of interested people to influence the development of education in certain directions (Jenkins and Shipman 1976).

Other bodies, organized for different purposes but having an additional and peripheral interest in education, also join in this national educational debate. The most obvious and influential of such bodies in the United Kingdom are the churches, whose contribution to the original establishment of public education was a great one, and who have, as a result, enjoyed a continuing influence on educational development since that time. Not only do the churches own and control schools and colleges themselves but they also exert a wider influence not least through their contribution to the training of teachers in the many colleges of education they have established and for which they remain responsible.

The influence of a country's economy on the curriculum is also clearly very important. Indeed, to a large extent it is to economic events and factors that one must look for an explanation of the development of most systems of education. Clearly one of the functions of the school system is to produce the manpower a country needs and this is a factor that cannot be ignored in curriculum planning. It would appear, however, that this kind of consideration does not usually lead to demands for increased vocational training in schools. On the contrary, the history, for example, of technical education in the United Kingdom reveals quite clearly that there are no really strong demands for this kind of provision. Nor are the present demands for a core curriculum couched in terms of increased vocational training, in spite of the fact that the needs of a technological society loom very large in the arguments adduced in support of this development. The demand seems rather to be for a good general education, a good grounding in the three Rs (Jenkins and Shipman 1976).

There are at least two reasons for this. The first is that most employers prefer to train their employees themselves. In this way they can provide them with the precise kind of training they need and supervise it themselves. Secondly, there is a need in a rapidly developing technological society for a force of workers who can adapt to changing techniques and this, as we have had cause to notice before, demands that the products of the educational system be educated to think for themselves so that they can adjust to and develop with the evolving technology itself.

Finally we must note the more formal and direct agencies of curriculum change. We have already discussed at some length the role of the examination boards in relation to curriculum development. We must also now recognize that there are other agencies exercising or attempting to exercise direct influence on the curriculum. Theories abound at national level concerning the most desirable forms of education and curriculum. Thus the publishers too exercise a serious influence on the curriculum by their decisions as to what to publish both in the field of theoretical discussions of education and of textbooks and other materials for use in schools.

A good deal of public money is also spent on research into education both within universities and colleges of education and under the auspices of more formally constituted research organizations such as the NFER. In the United Kingdom some of this multifarious activity was coordinated in 1963 by the establishment of the Schools Council which has since then stage-managed the production of over a hundred curriculum projects and would thus seem to be the most influential of those agencies concerned directly to promote curriculum development.

When we turn to a consideration of local influences on the curriculum, those that come most readily to mind are the direct influences on the schools exercised by those bodies and people responsible for the running of them. Where, as in the United Kingdom, ultimate responsibility for the financing and administration of schools rests with local government, a good deal of power would seem to reside with local government officers, although we must not forget that most of the money they have to spend on education comes from the central government in the form of a rate support grant.

How far this power extends to direct influence on the curriculum, however, is another matter. Certainly it is the task of the advisory staff to contribute to curriculum development. Equally certainly, as we continually mention, decisions made by those who hold the purse strings will often have important consequences for the curriculum. In practice the balance between professional and administrative interests is most obvious at this local level, the local politicians and education officers working in parallel with the advisers, and the teachers influencing organizational decisions either through their unions or by direct membership of certain advisory bodies.

The same sort of balance can also be seen in the constitution of the governing bodies of individual educational institutions, where again political and professional interests meet. This has been especially true since the recent introduction to many governing bodies of teacher, parent and, sometimes, student members. Technically, these are the bodies responsible for the curriculum of the school. In practice, however, in the United Kingdom they normally restrict their attentions to the general conduct of the school, leaving responsibility for the curriculum to the head teacher and thus to the school staff. Their power is, therefore, somewhat limited at present in its effect but potentially it is great (Jenkins and Shipman 1976) and the addition of more parent, teacher and student members might well help to unleash this potential force. Certainly, recent events, such as those at the William Tyndale school, which have led to attempts to tighten control over what the schools are doing, seem to be resulting also in a wider exercise of their powers by some governing bodies.

In the United Kingdom parents have until recently had little scope for influencing what goes on in schools, in spite of their obvious concern for the standard and kind of education their offsprings are receiving. Parent-teacher associations have tended to operate at the social level only and even when committees of parents have been organized by local authorities their influence has not been very great (Jenkins and Shipman 1976). In the U.S.A., however, the influence of parents on the curriculum is strong (Jenkins and Shipman 1976) and it may well be that now that they have direct access to the governing bodies of many schools in the United Kingdom their influence there will begin to increase. Certainly, if the potential power of the governing bodies is to be realized it is from this direction that the initial impetus is most likely to come.

It is this that gives interest to proposals currently under discussion in the United Kingdom to amend the constitution of governing bodies to make them more 'professional' by including a membership over half of which would be directly elected by parents and school staff, and by insisting that all governors, however elected, should be given a course of training which would include school administration, teaching methods, the curriculum and financial matters. Such a 'professional' governing body would then be given control of the school curriculum.

A development such as this would have the effect not only of giving the parents more 'say' in the affairs of the school and especially in curriculum matters, it would also perhaps put the kind of teeth into the governing body that we have suggested would enable it to become the most effective factor in curriculum change. It is essential, however, that teachers also be involved at this level, since, as we shall see later, in the last analysis they will decide what actually happens in the classroom. The suggestion that if governors are given this kind of control over the curriculum teachers should retain their professional responsibility for methods would seem to acknowledge this fact, but to try to separate the curriculum from the methods used to implement it in this way is to mis-understand totally the nature of the educational process. Teachers must either have autonomy in all aspects of the curriculum or they must be involved with others in all aspects of planning.

The constraints on the curriculum that operate within the school have been well documented by the Schools Council's research into Purpose, Power and Constraint in the Primary School Curriculum (Taylor et al. 1974) and they do to a large extent reflect a detailing of those practical considerations that, as we saw in Chapter 1, form an important element of Denis Lawton's model of curriculum planning.

The research team listed the constraints it regarded as important under three headings 'Constraints imposed by the human element (personal)', 'Organizational and administrative constraints' and 'Physical constraints' (Taylor et al. 1974). Among the former it included such things as the level of enthusiasm of teachers and their willingness to give time to any project, the level of their initial training and the in-service training provision available to them, the level and quality of support services from cleaning staff, clerical staff and ancillary classroom help. Among the organizational constraints it listed the form of organization in the school, the style of discipline, the form of the timetable, the size of classes, the age of the pupils and their home backgrounds. Finally, it outlined the physical constraints as:

a)   size and design of classrooms

b)   level of provision of storage space

c)   number of classrooms

d)   specialist facilities e.g. music room, laboratory, etc.

e)   form and style of school architecture.

(Taylor et al. 1974, p 80.)

Most teachers will readily recognize the significance of all of these factors in constraining any ambitions they may have for curriculum development. In addition we should also note how crucial is the availability of suitable resources of all kinds, including teachers with the appropriate skills and talents. There is no point in deciding on the idiosyncratic introduction of, say, Urdu into the curriculum if you have neither relevant resource materials nor a teacher with the necessary knowledge and expertise to teach it.

The curriculum of any given school, then, will be a product of all of these factors operating within the school and outside it at local and national level. The relative strengths of these influences and constraints will clearly vary according to each individual situation but the research project to which we have just referred did attempt to investigate, with interesting results, what teachers regard as being the most and the least influential of them in the primary school.

Among the most important points to emerge from this study were, firstly, the clear evidence that teachers — at least those who work in primary schools — see the in-school and other local influences as having far more bearing on what they do than anything that is done or said about education nationally, the government and the Secretary of State for Education and Science having little or no influence, especially when compared with the influence exercised by such factors as informal meetings of staff within the school. This bears out what has become apparent in other ways, namely the limited influence of most of the projects sponsored by bodies like the Schools Council (MacDonald and Walker 1976). In fact it is clear that when teachers set about curriculum change they do so from considerations of a very practical kind rather than as a result of detailed analysis of the theoretical issues involved (Taylor 1970) or of any national programme or guidelines they are offered.

The teacher will view the curriculum, then, from a different perspective from that of others concerned with curriculum development and will use the materials and ideas they produce to achieve his own ends rather than theirs. It is this characteristic of teachers that has resulted in the failure of most nationally developed curriculum projects to 'take' in the schools. Curriculum theory cannot ignore this.

A second interesting feature of curriculum development to emerge from this study is 'the confirmation that the school and the classroom are separate zones of influence; that the teacher has considerable *de facto* influence in the classroom, and not so much within the school, where the head, with his *de iure* power, has greatest influence' (Taylor et al. 1974, p. 64). The head is outstandingly the most influential factor in the school but the class teacher is regarded as more influential than the head when it comes to what goes on in individual classrooms.

Two further points arise from both of these findings. In the first place, it is clear where the gap is to be found that exists between the ideal and the real, the official and the actual, the formal and the operational curriculum, in other words between the theory and the practice of curriculum development. It will be equally clear, therefore, where effort and attention must be concentrated if this gap is to be closed. Secondly, it is also apparent that effective control of the real curriculum rests still with the teachers and we must recognize the role of the head and especially the classroom teacher in making all effective decisions about the curriculum. Teachers will do their own thing and no curriculum, no matter how carefully planned, will ever reach fruition unless the teachers are committed to it (Barker-Lunn 1970) and unless they understand its implications and the theoretical considerations underlying it. Again we must note the implications of this for a centralized curriculum.

This raises several issues that we must now turn to. The first of these is the difficulty of promoting the dissemination of curriculum innovation. The second is the resultant need to explore the problems and possibilities of supporting school-based curriculum development, of recognizing that ultimately the need is to help teachers to engage more effectively in developing the curriculum themselves. This in turn raises questions about the control of the curriculum and the problem of teacher-accountability which will lead us naturally into the discussing of the idea of a common core curriculum and a central monitoring of standards which will constitute the theme of our next and final chapter.

The dissemination of innovation

It is perhaps worth noting at the outset that it was the intention of the Schools Council from its inception to provide support for teachers in the development of the curriculum by extending the range of choices and variety of materials open to them. It chose to do this initially, however, by establishing national projects in certain areas of the curriculum and adopting a centre-periphery model of curriculum development (Schon 1971), hoping that the ideas for curriculum innovation that were developed centrally at the national level could be disseminated to the schools at the periphery and that each school could then be supported in its attempts to attend to its own developmental needs.

As we have seen, however, the inadequacies of this model have gradually become apparent. There is a wide gap between the ideas of a project held by its central planners and the realities of its implementation, if that is even the word, in the classroom by the teachers. Even when a project team sets out deliberately to support teachers in their own developments rather than to provide a teacher-proof blueprint (Shipman 1972), as was the case, for example, with the Humanities Curriculum Project, the Keele Integrated Studies project and the Goldsmiths' College Interdisciplinary Enquiry Project, the same difficulties have been experienced. It has proved impossible to get across to teachers the concept of the project, the theoretical considerations underlying it, in such a way as to ensure that these were reflected in its practice. And so a gap emerges between the ideals and the realities, a gap that in some cases is so wide as to negate the project entirely, at least in terms of the conception of it by its planners.

The main danger then becomes a possible loss of credibility for the project, a rejection of the theory behind it, if a malinformed or maladroit implementation of it derived from lack of adequate understanding has led to disastrous practical consequences. That something has not worked leads too readily to the assumption that it cannot work, rather than to a consideration of the possibility that one has messed it up. This has been especially apparent in the reaction of some secondary schools to the results of ill-thought-out attempts to introduce mixed-ability groupings.

Such a situation is clearly unsatisfactory since it means at one level that the large sums of money spent on central curriculum development are not producing anything like adequate returns and at a further level that they can be positively counter-productive, in so far as failures of this kind can lead to an entrenching of traditional positions.

Hence recent years have witnessed a good deal of attention given to the problems of the dissemination of curriculum innovation. In some cases this has led to little more than a determination to explore ways of promoting projects more positively, through improved in-service provision or closer involvement of the project team in the development of the work within the schools (Schools Council 1974b; MacDonald and Walker 1976). Others, however, have begun to identify some of the reasons for this failure of dissemination and to suggest that the model itself is wrong and that attention needs to be given to the development of alternative models.

Various hypotheses have been put forward to explain the inadequacies of the centre-periphery model of dissemination. One piece of research has indicated that even where a lot of positive effort has gone into promoting the dissemination of a project to the schools, barriers exist to its implementation in both the failure of teachers to perceive with clarity their new role and also the absence of conditions appropriate to their being able to acquire such a perception (Gross et al. 1971). 'Our analysis of the case study data led us to conclude that this condition could primarily be attributed to five circumstances: (1) the teachers' lack of clarity about the innovation; (2) their lack of the kinds of skills and knowledge needed to conform to the new role model; (3) the unavailability of required instructional materials; (4) the incompatibility of organizational arrangements with the innovation; and (5) lack of staff motivation' (Gross et al. 1971, p. 122). The first four of these conditions, they claim, existed from the outset; the last emerged later. Nor would this seem surprising.

It might be felt that some of the barriers listed here could be avoided with more careful preparation and support for teachers. Further difficulties, however, have been identified by those concerned with the dissemination of the Humanities Curriculum Project and here the problems of dissemination were most carefully considered in advance and detailed strategies for dissemination developed (Rudduck 1976). In particular, failure to achieve adequate dissemination was attributed to difficulties in communication between the project team and the schools (MacDonald and Rudduck 1971). It would be a mistake, however, to interpret that statement at too simple a level. For a number of features of this failure of communication have also been identified. One of these is the tendency of teachers 'to invest the development team with the kind of authority which can atrophy independence of judgement in individual school settings' (MacDonald and Rudduck 1971, p. 149). The converse of this was also observed, namely the anxiety of some teachers not to lose their own style by accepting too readily the specifications of method included in the project. Both of these factors would seem to point to the need for a full and proper involvement of the teachers with the development of the project.

Important here too is the manner in which innovations are introduced. It will be clear that if an innovation is to have chance of 'taking' in a school, it will be necessary for more to be done than the mere provision of resources and in-service support for teachers. Teachers will need to become committed to it, an ideological change will need to be promoted, if they are to be expected willingly to adapt their methods and approaches to meet the demands of the new work. This offers a far more subtle problem. It is here that the manner in which the proposed change is made becomes important. For if it is imposed by the head teacher, for example, or by powerful pressure from outside, the dictation involved will be counter-productive and will promote opposition and hostility in teachers rather than support. Not only will teachers in such circumstances not work to promote the change planned; they will quite often deliberately and actively sabotage the efforts of others. Again, some ill-advised attempts to introduce mixed-ability groupings in secondary schools provide us with very good and up-to-date examples of this.

It has further been suggested that this problem goes beyond a mere failure of communication or of the strategies employed to introduce the innovation and is in fact the result of the different views and definitions of a curriculum project that we have already suggested are taken by different bodies of people involved in it (Shipman 1972, 1973). The question must then be asked whose definition is to be seen as valid. To speak of dissemination or implementation, of the barriers to implementation created by schools and teachers, or of the need to improve the teachers' understanding of the theoretical considerations underlying a project is to make the assumption that it is the planner's view and definition that is to be accepted as valid. For this reason, it has been suggested that 'the process of curriculum dissemination, in so far as it assumes a stable message, does not occur. The process to which the term "dissemination" is conventionally applied would be more accurately described by the term "curriculum negotiation"' (MacDonald and Walker 1976, p. 43). In other words, having recognized that a gap exists between the ideals of the planners and the realities of the work of the teacher in the classroom, we should be concerned to close it by attempting not to bring the latter nearer to the former but to bring each closer to the other. To see the need to do this is to recognize that curriculum development is essentially a matter of local development, that it has to be school-based. It then becomes necessary to explain the ways in which the curriculum changes in individual educational institutions and how such change can be supported from without.

School-based curriculum development

One reason for considering the possibilities of school-based curriculum development, then, is that attempts at the dissemination of innovation by a centre-periphery model have met with little success. Another and more compelling reason, however, is that this is the only way of ensuring that curriculum change is in fact curriculum *development*. As

Malcolm Skilbeck says, school-based curriculum development 'provides more scope for the continuous adaptation of curriculum to individual pupil needs than do other forms of curriculum development' (Skilbeck 1976, pp. 93-4). Other systems are 'by their nature ill-fitted to respond to individual differences in either pupils or teachers. Yet these differences . . . are of crucial importance in learning. . . . At the very least, schools need greatly increased scope and incentive for adapting, modifying, extending and otherwise reordering externally developed curricula than is now commonly the case. Curriculum development related to individual differences must be a continuous process and it is only the school or school networks that can provide scope for this' (Skilbeck 1976, p. 94).

Such an approach will, of course, lead to great diversity and elsewhere Malcolm Skilbeck argues that curriculum diversity is essential if all pupils are to be given a meaningful educative experience (Skilbeck 1973). This is a point we have returned to many times throughout this book, the need for teachers to be able to devise programmes of work tailored to what they can recognize as the requirements of their own individual pupils. If education is to be meaningful to all pupils and if all are to have truly educative experiences, then it is only by allowing for this local development at the level of the school that this is likely to be achieved, so that we must accept the diversity of provision it entails. In any case, as we claimed when discussing the idea of common principles of education in Chapter 2, it will not be at the level of educational principles that this diversity is likely to occur but at the level of content where, as we argued earlier, at least if we concern ourselves only with educational considerations, it is of less significance.

For these reasons, then, the only satisfactory curriculum development is likely to be school-based curriculum development and we must now consider what this entails.

We have referred before to the fact that some curriculum change in schools can be attributed to nothing more positive than the unplanned 'drift' that results from the action of the pressures we discussed in the first part of this chapter (Hoyle 1969a). The cause/effect relationships existing between these pressures and such relatively unplanned curriculum change provide an interesting area of study. Our concern here, however, is with curriculum development, planned curriculum change, so that our main interest is in discovering the conditions which are likely to be most conducive to promoting deliberate attempts at curriculum innovation in school. Two broad kinds of question emerge from this consideration. Firstly, we need to ask what conditions within the school are likely to be most conducive to curriculum innovation. Secondly, we need to explore the most appropriate form in which assistance and support can be offered from outside the school.

We have mentioned several times how crucial it is that a curriculum innovation should '"take" with the school and become fully institutionalised' (Hoyle 1969b, p. 230). It has further been suggested that whether this is likely to happen or not will depend on the organizational health of the institution, since only a healthy institution can readily absorb a new development. As Eric Hoyle goes on to say, 'the central problem facing the curriculum development movement is the avoidance of tissue rejection whereby an innovation does not "take" with a school because the social system of the school is unable to absorb it into its normal functioning' (Hoyle 1969b, p. 231).

But what criteria are we to use to define a healthy institution? We face immediately the kinds of difficulty that surround concepts of mental health, namely those that arise from the values that must be implicit in any definition we offer. On the other hand, although much more work needs to be done in this area, there are some indications of what factors are relevant to the question of a school's ability to digest satisfactorily a curriculum innovation.

The style of the head teacher is clearly crucial, since the organizational structure he creates within the school will be of great significance to the reaction of teachers to proposed curriculum change (Halpin 1966, 1967; Hoyle 1969b). The degree to which a school is 'open' is also very important (Halpin 1966, 1967; Bernstein 1967; Hoyle 1969b). The more open a school is the more likely it is to be able to absorb innovation. For an 'open' school will offer teachers a greater degree of freedom and autonomy and will encourage a higher level of collaboration between them. They are thus more likely to have the confidence that change requires and to have been involved themselves in the processes of change. As we have mentioned several times, no kind of change will 'take' if it is not accepted by the teacher at the coal-face. In the last resort, therefore, his motivation is paramount and this is most likely to be high if he feels himself to be completely involved and, indeed, in control of events.

In more detail, the investigation into the 38 schools that were involved in the Schools Council's Integrated Studies Project based at Keele led to the following rather tentative suggestions as to the main characteristics of a school that is ready for innovation. 'The salient points are that the school which is likely to introduce and implement successfully a planned innovation would:

— have teachers who would feed back information to the project

— have teachers who would accumulate supplementary material

— have teachers who had volunteered knowing that they would be involved in a lot of work

— reorganise its timetable to provide planning time for teachers involved in innovation

— have a headteacher who supported the innovation but did not insist on being personally involved

— have a low staff turnover among key personnel

— be free of any immediate need to reorganise as part of a changing local school situation.'

(Shipman 1973, p 53.)

To this list one might add also a further point that emerged from an exploration of the difficulties of dissemination associated with the Humanities Curriculum Project. 'It seems that an experiment settles well in a school where teachers are confronting a problem and contemplating action. The experiment should extend the range of their strategies for dealing with the problem' (MacDonald and Rudduck 1971, pp. 150/1). If the teachers are aware of a need, then, and the climate of the school gives them the confidence and support to experiment with possible solutions to that need, a project has a far better chance of succeeding.

These, then, are some of the characteristics of the school as a social system that will help to decide whether it is ready for curriculum innovation or not. There are besides, of course, a good many considerations of a more practical kind relating to the geography of the school, the availability of appropriate resources and such like. In the last resort, however, it is the social climate that will be crucial and it is on this that we must concentrate if we wish to develop strategies of curriculum change within the school.

On the other hand, it might be argued that if a school does in fact have all of these characteristics there is hardly any point in trying to get it to change (Shipman 1973). Certainly, it does raise the question of how far such an institution needs an outside curriculum developer or what form of outside support it can profit from and we must now turn to a consideration of that.

The first point that should perhaps be made in answer to these questions is, of course, that for those schools which do not enjoy the characteristics we have just listed, if the advantages of planned curriculum change are not to be denied them, strategies must be developed for bringing about the conditions that will make curriculum development possible for them. This is one reason why we need to understand more than we do both about what these conditions are and about how they can be promoted. This is clearly an area in which support from outside the school is needed, although how it can be provided is more difficult to decide.

Secondly, any school engaged in any kind of curriculum innovation will need a good deal of support of a practical kind. At one level this will mean financial support and the provision of resources of all kinds. Such support can be offered by the local authority especially, perhaps, through the facilities of its teachers' centres.

Some schools have recently made senior appointments of teachers with special responsibility for coordinating and guiding curriculum — curriculum coordinators or curriculum development officers. This is a practice which has much to recommend it. It is a step towards achieving that kind of coordinated development across the curriculum which we said in Chapter 1 was often lacking, especially in secondary schools where the tradition has been for development to go on within individual subjects in isolation from each other. It also ensures that there is one person in the school who can be expected to attempt to organize support from outside agencies for any group of teachers engaged in any particular innovative activity. Such a person can also act as a focus for curriculum study groups in the school, an innovation which is essential if teachers are to be made fully aware of what is entailed in school-based curriculum development.

However, if we have been right to identify the teacher in the classroom as the hub of all this activity and the person whose role is quite fundamental and crucial, the most important need will be for adequate support for him or her. It becomes increasingly important for his initial course of training to have prepared him to take this central role in curriculum development. It becomes even more important, however, that he be given adequate opportunities for continuing in-service education to enable him to obtain any new skills that the innovations require of him and a developing insight into the wider issues of education, a deep understanding of which is vital for any kind of adequate planning, research or development.

This is why major curriculum changes such as the introduction of mixed ability groupings in secondary schools have worked most smoothly and effectively when, as in the West Riding of Yorkshire under Sir Alec Clegg's guidance, suitable in-service courses have been made available on demand and tailored not to the advisory staff's ideas of what is needed but to what the teacher themselves ask for (Kelly 1975). It is for the same reason that where national projects have developed training courses for teachers wishing to make use of the project materials, teachers who have had this training achieve more success than those who have not (Elliott and Adelman 1973).

In short, there can be no curriculum development without teacher development and the more teachers are to be given responsibility for curriculum development the more important it becomes that they be given all possible support of this kind. The potential of the role of the professional tutor as the focal point of this kind of teacher development, linking initial and in-service teacher education and developing contacts between the school and colleges and other institutions responsible for these courses has so far not been fully appreciated but it offers opportunities that may be crucial to school-based curriculum development (Kelly 1973). It is very important, therefore, that teachers be put in touch with any outside agency that can provide them with the resources, the skills or the understanding they need if they are to take responsibility for developing the curriculum.

Another aspect of this kind of support for teachers is that with which the Ford Teaching Project has concerned itself. As part of the help teachers need with innovation they need assistance with the monitoring of what they are doing in the classroom. We have already referred briefly in Chapter 5 to the attempts of the Ford Teaching Project to support teachers in developing the skills needed to make reasonably objective appraisals of their own work, to engage in 'research-based teaching'. Without some kind of evaluation any curriculum innovation becomes meaningless and probably also impossible. If teachers are to take responsibility for curriculum development they need to be able to monitor their own work in this way in order to provide themselves with appropriate data for continued curriculum development. We also saw in Chapter 5 the emerging notion of a process model of evaluation, of evaluation as action research. One of the main purposes of the Ford Teaching Project was 'to help teachers by fostering an action-research orientation towards classroom problems' (Elliott and Adelman 1973, p. 10). This is offered as an alternative to the model of action research in which researchers from outside come into the classroom and work with the teacher. It is felt that this kind of relationship erodes the teacher's autonomy and that if this is to be protected he must be enabled to take responsibility for his own action research as part of his responsibility for his own curriculum development (Elliott and Adelman 1973). This the Ford Teaching Project has attempted to encourage.

What about the curriculum developer, then? Is there a place for a professional curriculum developer if curriculum development is to be school-based? It is still not clear what role there is for the outside expert. This was a second-order action research project for the Ford Teaching Project team. At the same time as helping teachers to develop the ability to engage in their own 'research-based teaching', they wanted also to explore how best this kind of teaching can be assisted from outside. Unfortunately, little of value has emerged so far on this issue.

The logic of the Ford Teaching Project's approach would seem to be that, once teachers have acquired a research-based teaching orientation as part of their basic weaponry, the need for outside support will disappear, so that perhaps the role of the curriculum developer is to be seen as provisional only, his services being needed only until such times as teachers themselves have acquired his skills.

Two questions, however, must be asked before we too readily accept such a view. In the first place, we must ask how far the average teacher is likely to be able to develop the abilities this will require of him. Apart from the problem of adding yet another chore to his already heavy task, we saw in Chapter 5 that it has not been easy for the Ford Teaching Project team to develop in teachers the detachment and the security of confidence necessary to be able to make reasonably objective appraisals of their work, although the team did express optimism on this point.

Secondly, however, we must also ask whether there will not always be a need for someone to come from the outside to take a detached view of what is being done and to suggest possible alternatives. Few of us cannot profit from this kind of second opinion. Perhaps this is to be seen as a function of teachers from other schools as part of the process of moderation that we suggested should be an essential element in all assessment procedures. But there may also continue to be a need for someone acting as a professional consultant, a role that members of the advisory services should perform. It is interesting to note that these were the two main features of the work of the Goldsmiths' College Curriculum Laboratory from its inception. It brought teachers together not for in-service courses but to give them the opportunity to share problems and solutions with each other. At the same time it provided them with opportunities for consultation with experts in whatever fields they decided were relevant and useful to them. Subsequently too it attempted to provide schools with consultancy facilities.

Perhaps there is still a role then for the wandering expert in curriculum development. If there is, and only subsequent research will answer that question for us, it is likely that that role will be to provide teachers with expert advice and the detached appraisal they cannot provide themselves and not to arrive hawking his own pet project, cobbled together in a place somewhat removed from the realities of any particular group of classrooms. His job will be to follow and serve the teachers rather than to lead them into his own new pastures. He can only support curriculum development; he will no longer attempt to direct it.

Summary and conclusions

In this chapter we have tried to locate the central issues of curriculum development in the social context of the school and society. We have done this by examining some of the influences and constraints, including those exercised by the system of public examinations, that act upon the curriculum from both within and without the school, by considering the difficulties of disseminating national curriculum projects and the problems of providing suitable support for school-based curriculum development. Our final conclusion was that the focal point of all curriculum development worthy of the name is the teacher in the classroom and that in the last analysis he must hold the reins of curriculum development in his hands.

However, not everyone is happy at the idea that teachers should have this central role in curriculum development, although all the evidence is that if they do not then nothing that can really be styled development is likely to occur. There are those who would claim that decisions about the curriculum should be made from outside and that control of the curriculum should not be left to the teacher, a claim that acquires impetus with every educational failure that reaches the attention of the public through the national press but does not seem to lose its force from a consideration of all the educational successes that the national press seldom informs its readers about. Freedom and autonomy for teachers has led to the development of schools like Summerhill, as well as those like William Tyndale, and we forget that at our peril.

Direct central control of the curriculum is something we have not witnessed in the United Kingdom for many years. In the early days of the development of a state system of education grants from central government were conditional on the results of inspection; 'payment by results' represented another kind of attempt to ensure that the work of the schools was effectively controlled by the paymasters, although in this case it was local rather than central control.

Indirect influences, of course, continue to exist, as we mentioned earlier in this chapter. The dependence of every local authority on its rate support grant will ensure that it cannot do too much that might be in direct opposition to the policy of the central government, as has been clear in recent disputes between some local authorities and the central government concerning the comprehensivization of secondary education. We have already referred also to the implications of large-scale organizational changes for the curriculum of the school.

We have also noted, however, that there is little or no direct control exercised over the curriculum itself. Slowly, during the years of state-provided education in the United Kingdom, this control has been eroded. The handbooks and even syllabuses once produced by central and local government officers have been replaced by more general advisory documents and the role of the inspectorate at both local and central levels, as we have seen, has changed to an advisory one (Jenkins and Shipman 1976). The only direct external control on the curriculum that still remains is the public examination system and, as we have also seen, recent developments towards greater teacher control are tending to minimize the effectiveness of that as an external check on the curriculum.

Current demands for a common curriculum, however, represent a reaction against this, a concern expressed about the implications of such increased autonomy for teachers and a desire to reassert the control from outside that has been slowly lost. This movement has taken root in the United States and in 1974 forty states were attempting to establish legal requirements for teacher accountability (Hamilton 1976). It represents an attempt to apply business efficiency methods and criteria to the evaluation of the work of schools and teachers and usually takes the form of establishing state-wide objectives for schools and tests to measure their standards of achievement. To this extent it is a movement which reflects an attempt to re-establish control over the schools, and especially the curriculum, of a kind that, as we have just seen, has not been witnessed in the United Kingdom nor in the United States for some years. It is thus an attempt to put back the clock and to reverse or at least slow down the trend towards increased teacher and school autonomy that we have noted throughout this book.

What happens in the United States today does tend to be repeated in the United Kingdom tomorrow and we have recently seen a growing demand in Britain for a similar form of accountability. For the notion of a centralized core to the curriculum which has attracted the attention of many politicians, including the Prime Minister himself, in recent months and has had much support from industrialists and employers generally, is essentially a demand for centralized control over the curriculum of the schools and a central monitoring of standards of attainment in certain specific fields. Linked with this demand is the establishment of the Assessment of Performance Unit by the Department of Education and Science and the beginning of an attempt to re-establish the power and the role of the inspectorate.

The implications of this movement for what we have said so far about curriculum development are sweeping and we must turn in our next and final chapter to a detailed examination of some of the more important of them, since such demands do represent an attempt to deprive teachers of that degree of autonomy which we have argued is crucial to adequate curriculum development and an attempt to return to the system of former times, which, in the opinion of many judges, was more effective in inhibiting than in promoting such development.

CHAPTER 7

A COMMON CURRICULUM

The central role in curriculum development that we assigned in Chapter 6 to the teacher has direct relevance, as we pointed out, for an issue that has recently attracted a great deal of interest in the United Kingdom at all levels from that of the Prime Minister downwards (or upwards according to the view you take of relative status). That issue is the question of whether decisions about the curriculum or, at least, the core elements of the curriculum, should be taken centrally, whether there should be a common curriculum, established centrally and imposed on all schools financed by the state.

This is an issue that has many theoretical implications of a very wide kind and it is certainly one that picks up and links together many of the points that we have endeavoured to examine in earlier chapters of this book. Thus a discussion of the problems and implications of this notion of establishing by central control a common curriculum or a common core to the curriculum will effectively round off our exploration of the theory and practice of curriculum development, since it will draw many threads together and will, as a result, act as a summary to the book as a whole.

The background

It is perhaps worth reminding ourselves from the outset that the United Kingdom has been hitherto an exception in allowing its teachers and head teachers the degree of freedom over the curriculum of their schools that they currently enjoy. We have already noted the hidden constraints and influences that they are subject to in this respect and we have commented on the fact that, as a result of these, the most interesting features of the curricula of most schools in the United Kingdom are their similarities rather than their differences. Nevertheless, the fact remains that legally there is no binding requirement on any school to include any particular subject or activity in its curriculum other than a weekly period of religious instruction.

This freedom contrasts most markedly with the procedures in other countries, most of which lay down in varying degrees of detail essential requirements for the curriculum of all schools. Thus there is a core curriculum established for the 10-Year School in the USSR which sets out the range of subjects to be included for each year group and also lists the number of hours that are to be devoted to each every week. Nor does this requirement leave much scope for the addition of other subjects at the discretion of the individual school, since very little of the working week is left to provide any such latitude. This scheme has provided the basic model for the curriculum of all Eastern block countries.

A similar approach to curriculum control can be seen also in most Western European countries. There are, of course, variations in the degree of control. Not all countries, for example, specify the number of hours to be devoted to each area; some leave rather more time for optional areas of study; there is some variation in the extent of the control that is exercised in relation to different age-groups of children; and sometimes, as in West Germany, for example, more than one common curriculum is established to cater for children of different intellectual abilities. However, the principle of central control over what are seen as the most important areas of the curriculum is well-established and almost unquestioned outside the United Kingdom.

However, in the United Kingdom the tradition has been very different and the idea that there should be a common curriculum for all pupils is a comparatively recent one. To some extent it is an idea that has followed in the wake of the wider notion of education for all. There is no logical connection between the idea of education for all and that of a common curriculum, nor do demands for educational equality imply that all must have the same educational diet, since, as the Plowden Report asserted, there is no incompatibility between the idea of equality of educational opportunity and variety of educational provision (Downey and Kelly 1975). Originally, therefore, the ideal of education for all, as it was expressed in the 1944 Education Act, was interpreted as requiring not that all should have the same educational provision but that the content of education should vary according to such considerations as age, aptitude and ability.

This was a natural development of what can be discerned throughout the history of the growth of the educational system of the United Kingdom, since this has been characterized from the beginning by the development of two or more separate curricula, those of the grammar and of the elementary schools and later of the grammar, technical (where they existed) and the modern schools. Again we note the dead hand of Plato manipulating us still in the twentieth century and encouraging us to see education as having at least two forms, one for the able and another for the less able.

As a result we find many actually criticizing the work of the secondary modern schools in the 1940s and 1950s on the grounds that they were 'aping the grammar schools' by setting up a curriculum that appeared to be for the most part no more than a watered down version of the grammar school curriculum. Equally, however, it is not surprising to find them doing this, since the inadequacies and inaccuracies of the selection procedures employed, well-documented in many research studies of the time, make it clear that even if the generation of two or more curricula is in itself justified, the practical implementation of these, and especially the matching of pupils to them, is far from clear-cut and easy.

Problems of selection, then, are the focus of the criticisms that have been levelled at the tripartite selective system of secondary education, but these have also been accompanied by charges of unfairness and inequality which have resulted in the ending of selection and the replacement of that system by a pattern of comprehensive secondary education, a movement which would seem to imply a need for some commonality of educational provision. Thus we find the claim now being made that, if justice and fairness are to be attained and the ideal of education for all achieved, all pupils should have access to the same areas or bodies of knowledge and learning.

Recent years, then, have seen an increase in the educational and social arguments adduced in favour of the establishment of a common core to the curriculum and to these, of late, have been added certain political and economic arguments. These have derived some strength and force from particular cases in which the freedom of the teachers to develop their own curricula appears to have been abused or, at least, to have resulted in some educational failure, and events of this kind, as we have already seen, have in turn strengthened the hands of those who have felt for some time that educational provision ought to be more firmly in the control of people outside the teaching profession.

On the other hand, we have traced in the earlier chapters of this book some of the ways in which curriculum development has been forwarded precisely because of this freedom that teachers in the United Kingdom enjoy and, indeed, we have tried to make out a case for asserting that this is the only basis for real curriculum development. We have claimed that it is the teacher who is ultimately responsible for what is actually done in the classroom and that the only way in which we can ensure that the curriculum continues to develop is by recognizing the central role of the teacher and seeking ways of supporting curriculum development of a school-based kind. In making these claims, however, we did acknowledge the concern felt by some over the need for teachers to be accountable so that we can appreciate that it is from that kind of concern that demands for some central control over part of the curriculum stem.

We must now consider, therefore, first the arguments for such central control and then some of the difficulties it might create, in order to attempt to resolve the dilemma with which we appear to be faced.

The case for a common core to the curriculum

Broadly speaking, three kinds of argument are produced in favour of the idea of a common curriculum and all of these we have touched upon already. First of all, we have those philosophical or epistemological arguments that base their recommendations for the content of a common curriculum on particular views about the nature of knowledge. Secondly, we have certain social or sociological arguments which base their case on either a sociological assessment of what society and its culture are or certain ideological claims about what they ought to be. Finally, as a kind of subvariant of this, we have the political or economic arguments which claim that the curriculum should be planned in such a way as to ensure that all pupils have the opportunity to develop to a certain standard the skills and knowledge that will enable them to meet the demands of a technological society.

One kind of argument, then, claims that since certain kinds of knowledge have a status and value superior to others they have a prior claim for inclusion in any curriculum that is to be regarded as educational in the full sense. We have already noted the claim of Richard Peters that education is concerned only with those activities which have an intrinsic value (Peters 1965, 1966). To this we might add the theory of Paul Hirst, which we discussed in Chapter 4, that knowledge is to be divided into seven or eight discrete forms of rationality, each distinguishable from the other through its unique logical structure, and of education as the initiation of pupils into all of these forms (Hirst 1965). If this is the view that one takes of education, then it will follow that the curriculum for all pupils must consist of these intrinsically worthwhile activities and of all of these forms of knowledge or understanding (Hirst 1969; Hirst and Peters 1970). On this kind of argument any pupil whose curriculum excludes him from any of these areas of human knowledge and understanding is being offered an educational provision that is by definition inferior or is not receiving an education in the full sense at all.

The sociological version of this same argument is the one we have already noted that is based on the idea that it is the job of the school to transmit the culture of the society and that the curriculum must be designed to convey what is worthwhile in the culture of the society to all pupils.

This is the kind of consideration that has formed the basis of the cases that have been made out hitherto for a common core to the curriculum. These are John White's major reasons, for example, for suggesting that the essential elements of the compulsory curriculum at secondary level should be communication, mathematics, the physical sciences, art appreciation and philosophical thought (White 1973). The same kinds of consideration too underlie Denis Lawton's recommendation that the curriculum should contain six core areas — five disciplines and one interdisciplinary unit. The six areas he suggests are mathematics, the physical and biological sciences, the humanities and social sciences (including history, geography, classical studies, social studies, literature, film and TV and religious studies), the expressive and creative arts, moral education and interdisciplinary work (Lawton 1969, 1973, 1975).

This kind of argument for a common curriculum, then, is based on those particular views of knowledge and of society that we considered earlier in this book and on the belief that it is possible to establish some kind of value system that will enable us to choose what is worthwhile in knowledge and in the culture of the society.

The social arguments for a common curriculum start, as it were, from the opposite end of things. For they begin by considering some of the implications of not offering a common form of education to everyone. They have been prompted by recent attempts to base education on the interests of children, to try to make school-work meaningful and relevant to them by planning it in relation to their experience of their own immediate environment. The suggestion made by the Schools Council's Working Paper No. 11, for example, that we might base the education of pupils in part on the experience to be gained from a study of 'the 97 bus' (Schools Council 1967) was particularly effective in sparking off this kind of reaction. For it is claimed that an approach such as this can lead to a form of social control every bit as sinister as the imposition of one culture or one set of values on all (White 1968, 1973). If a child's experience is to be limited to his own culture, his own environment, what he is already familiar with before he enters school, then there is a real risk that he will be trapped in that cultural environment and given little opportunity of gaining experience outside it.

Furthermore, if we once concede that two or three curricula might be generated to meet two or three broadly different kinds of need, we are almost certainly accepting implicitly the idea that Plato made quite explicit, that education in the full sense is only capable of being achieved by some gifted people and that the rest must be offered something inferior, which can only be some form of indoctrination or 'education in obedience'.

These social arguments for a common core to the curriculum, then, will need to be looked at very closely.

Finally, to these epistemological, sociological and social arguments has recently been added the political and economic case. As we suggested earlier, this movement received its initial impetus from events in several schools where it has been felt that teachers have abused their freedom and autonomy and that as a result their pupils have missed out in certain important respects. This kind of unfortunate occurrence could be avoided, it is felt, if more direct control were exercised over what is done in schools.

There are two facets to this argument and it will be helpful if we can distinguish them, since they derive from two kinds of concern that have been expressed, one over the content of what is taught in schools and the relative proportions of time allocated to different kinds of activity, the second concerning the standard of attainment reached by pupils in certain specific areas, particularly literacy and numeracy.

Concern over the content of what is taught has been expressed by those who believe that the schools are not producing enough people who have been trained in such a way as to meet the demands of a techno- logical society for scientists and technologists. Too many pupils, it is claimed, are exercising the choices offered them by schools and universities to pursue interests in the humanities or in the social sciences and too few are opting for advanced work in the physical and natural sciences. The only solution that it is felt can be found for this state of affairs is to decree centrally that pupils shall not have such choices and to insist that all have a larger scientific and/or techno- logical component than at present in their curriculum. This, of course, reflects the approach that we have already briefly referred to as adopted in the USSR where there is no doubt that the prime consideration in establishing a central core to the curriculum is the economic needs of society.

The concern for standards of attainment has a somewhat different thrust. For its main preoccupation is not so much with establishing what shall be taught in schools as in monitoring the standards attained in what is taught and especially in those areas of the curriculum which are common to all schools — the basic skills of reading, writing and computation. The point here, then, is not so much that teachers cannot be left to choose the right sorts of activity for their pupils as that they cannot be trusted to ensure that sufficiently high standards are attained unless there is some kind of outside supervision. Thus we hear again demands for greater teacher accountability. To this end the Schools Council is being asked to reduce the extent of teacher control over its activities. An Assessment of Performance Unit has been established by the Department of Education and Science. And it is the intention to strengthen, or rather to reassert, the powers of the inspectorate, to give it back its teeth or to provide it with new, presumably false, ones.

All of these arguments appear to have some force, but it will also be apparent that many of them cut across not only most of what has been said earlier in this book but also what we have tried to identify as the whole trend of curriculum development in recent years in the United Kingdom towards an increasingly school-based model and away from this centre-periphery model, the inadequacies of which we attempted to expose in Chapter 6.

We must now consider, therefore, some of the problems and difficulties that this notion of a centralized core curriculum raises.

Problems and difficulties

In so far as many of the arguments offered in support of the idea of a common curriculum derive from certain views about the nature of knowledge and of values, we need do no more than remind ourselves of the difficulties of this kind of argument which we examined in some detail in Chapter 3, when discussing this same question of the basis upon which we can decide upon the content of the curriculum. For we noted then that there is a variety of positions one can take on this issue of the nature of knowledge and that among the least convincing of these is that which claims some kind of objective status for knowledge. Even less convincing, we claimed, are those arguments which attempt to demonstrate the superiority of certain kinds of knowledge and human activity over others. If we were right to argue there that there is no firm foundation upon which we can establish the prior claims of some areas of human knowledge and activity to be included in the curriculum, then that same argument has even more force in the context of proposals to establish a common curriculum for all pupils.

This becomes immediately apparent when we ask what is to be the content of such a common curriculum and who shall have the right to decide on it. For even if we agree in principle that some of the arguments for a commonality of basic educational provision are strong, such agreement immediately breaks down when we come to decide what such basic provision should consist of and who is to be the arbiter.

Who shall decide? Shall it be the teachers and other educationists? Shall it be the philosophers or the sociologists? Shall it be the politicians or the parents or even the children themselves? It might be argued that in practice all of these groups of people currently contribute to curriculum planning, but to say that any one group or even all of them collectively should decide on the content of a compulsory common curriculum for all pupils is to go far beyond current practice and even, perhaps, beyond common sense.

The same kind of problem emerges when we consider what the content of such a curriculum should be. Again, even if the idea is accepted in principle, further difficulties arise when we undertake the impossible task of reaching agreement on its content. What is it that all pupils should be introduced to as part of their education? Those proposals that have been put forward for the content of such a curriculum are far from indisputable. For they are derived, as we have seen, either from a particular view of the nature of knowledge or from some idea of what is valuable in the culture of society or some attempt at combining both of these considerations (White 1973; Lawton 1969, 1973, 1975). John White's suggestion, for example, that the compulsory curriculum at secondary level should consist primarily of communication, mathematics, the physical sciences, art appreciation and philosophical thought would hardly have universal acceptance. The idea of compulsory philosophical thought for some of the classes many teachers meet each day in their secondary schools is likely to be particularly productive of wry smiles or even hollow laughter. There is probably no single activity that will have universal support in its claims for inclusion in a common core of the curriculum. Even the teaching of reading has been described and criticized as a subversive activity that schools should not promote (Postman 1970).

The converse of this is also true. For just as there will be minority views opposed to the inclusion even of those things that have almost universal acceptance, there will also be those minority interests that will be vociferously demanding the inclusion of those things that they themselves happen for personal reasons to be committed to. A good example of this is the demand being made at the political level for the inclusion of religious instruction of some kind in the common core. Once the principle of a common core curriculum is accepted, such idiosyncratic demands will proliferate and thus render its implementation almost impossible.

Thus the establishment of a common curriculum must founder on the practical issues of what should be included in it and who shall decide on this.

To these problems that derive from the difficulty, even the impossibility, of establishing any universally accepted criteria for judging the relative worth of different kinds of knowledge, we must add the further difficulties that are raised by the criticisms currently being made of the content of the curriculum by many sociologists (Young 1971). For, as we have seen, their claims that all knowledge must be recognized as being socially constructed lead not only to an awareness of the lack of such objective criteria; they also raise further issues of a more sinister kind concerning the likely results of imposing a common system of knowledge on all pupils.

For, as we saw in Chapter 3, it is argued that knowledge is socially constructed, that culture is impossible to define, that many cultures can be identified in a modern pluralist society and that to impose one culture, one set of values on all pupils regardless of their origins, their social class, race or creed is to risk at best offering them a curriculum that is irrelevant, meaningless and alienating and at worst using the educational system as a means of effecting an inhibiting form of social control (Young 1971).

It is claimed, therefore, that such a process results in the attempt to introduce children to areas of knowledge that they find irrelevant to their own lives and meaningless in relation to their own experience and thus encourages them to reject what they are offered, so that it leads not to education but to disaffection and even alienation from both the content of education and society itself. Further, as an attempt to impose a particular value system on pupils, it is difficult to defend such practice even from the charge of indoctrination, so that such a system is not only inefficient and counter-productive, it is also open to criticism on moral grounds.

Further support for such a view has come from the activities of those who have been attempting in practice to develop programmes of work that would be relevant and meaningful to pupils and would as a result encourage in them a fuller and therefore more educational involvement in their work. Thus, as we have already noted, recent years have seen an accelerating movement at all levels of education towards 'progressive', 'pupil-centred' methods, heuristic approaches of all kinds, learning by experience, learning by discovery, learning through interests and so on. The general trend of this movement, as we have seen, has been towards a greater individualization of education.

Thus we have the strange situation that the idea of a common educational provision which is argued for on grounds of equality, justice and fairness is opposed most vigorously for precisely the same reasons by those who might be regarded as on the 'left wing' of educational debate, those who see the imposition of knowledge as a form of social control and those who even go so far as to advocate total de-schooling.

We are, therefore, presented with yet another dilemma, or rather with evidence that we are faced by a debate about means rather than ends. For on both sides we have a commitment to the the ideal of educational equality but we are faced with a headlong clash on the question of how such an ideal is to be achieved, whether by insisting that all pupils have access to the same knowledge or by tailoring educational provision to suit their individual needs. This is a point we must return to later.

In the meantime, we must proceed to note that none of these arguments deriving from problems over the nature of knowledge will affect to the slightest degree the political and economic arguments for a common core curriculum. For the case there for the inclusion of certain kinds of knowledge and activity in the curriculum of all pupils is based not on educational or epistemological arguments for the intrinsic value or superiority of these areas of knowledge; it is based entirely on grounds of their social utility and importance. What other grounds could there be for insisting that pupils should be discouraged from spending too much of their time pursuing their interests in the humanities and social sciences and should be required to devote more time to science and technology?

This kind of argument, however, does present some difficulties of its own. In the first place, it raises many issues concerning the rights of individual pupils and parents to choose the content of their education, to decide for themselves or for their children what their interests are and what they wish to spend their time pursuing. We considered in Chapter 3 in some detail the problems and possibilities of basing our curriculum on the interests of pupils. Such a practice clearly will become impossible, except in the limited and perhaps unacceptable sense of using their interests to further the purposes of other people, if we accept that the content of their education is to be decided, even in part, from without. Thus an opportunity to develop an educational provision for each pupil that might be meaningful to him in his own terms will be lost and at the same time his freedom to choose for himself will be infringed beyond any point that can be justified on educational grounds. For it is one thing to attempt to justify requiring pupils to engage in certain kinds of learning activity on the grounds that we believe this will be good for them; it is quite another to justify it as being good for society. Is Plato creeping up on us again?

Secondly the politicians and the economists are likely to encounter at least as much difficulty in reaching agreement on the content of a common core curriculum as we suggested the educationists, the epistemologists and the culture-theorists would experience. There are several levels at which this will become apparent.

To begin with, as we have already suggested, beyond the need for basic literacy and numeracy, there is likely to be a good deal of disagreement. We have already referred to the attempt by certain politicians to have religious instruction included in the central core as a prime example of the disputes that will immediately follow the acceptance in principle of a common core curriculum. Any list of subjects produced will reflect the personal preferences and values of the person who compiles it. Secondly, even if attention is concentrated on standards in the basic skills, it is difficult to know how a clear standard can be set or what such a standard would mean. Thirdly, there will be further difficulties in determining what is meant by the demand for such things as adequate scientific and technological education. Does this mean theoretical understanding or practical expertise? Does it suggest that we concentrate on developing children's knowledge of what happens and how it can be controlled or of why it happens (Fowler 1977). As George Fowler says, 'Any attempt to determine the content of an acceptable core curriculum by listing subjects is doomed to failure. The list must be either unduly restrictive, or so all-embracing as to tax the wits of the most sophisticated timetabler and the energies of the most dedicated pupil' (Fowler 1977).

This raises a further point concerning the degree of commonality we should be aiming for. We noted at the beginning of this chapter the variations in this that can be observed in those countries that have a centralized curriculum. How far are we to go in specifying centrally what should be taught in all schools? Is it enough to produce a list of subjects or do we need also to devise central syllabuses? Should there be some central dictation of the methods to be used? Certainly some of the recent events in schools that have acquired national significance have been the result of the methods adopted rather than the subjects being taught. Are we to specify the number of hours each week to be devoted to each subject or even the times of the day when they are to be taught? Are we to prescribe textbooks to be used by all schools in the teaching of these subjects at particular levels and to particular age-groups?

All of these would seem to follow logically upon the demand for commonality. For if we leave teachers too much scope for individual interpretation then very little that can be described as common will ensue. We have already noted several times the gap that exists between the official and the actual curriculum of any school or individual classroom. That gap will be even greater if there is central dictation of content but latitude for local interpretation of such things as time to be spent on each subject, methods to be employed, approaches to be adopted and textbooks to be used. A consideration of the wide range of interpretation of the present requirement in the United Kingdom for a compulsory period of religious instruction for all pupils will illustrate effectively the point that is being made.

The same kind of difficulty is inherent in the proposal we considered in Chapter 6 that is currently under discussion in the United Kingdom for giving school governing bodies control over the curriculum while leaving to the teacher decisions as to the teaching methods to be used, on the grounds that these are his or her professional responsibility. Even if we allow for the fact that the governing bodies would be redesigned to give a majority of members elected by parents and teachers and that all governors would be trained for their task, an arrangement of this kind creates a distinction between content and method which is not only undesirable but also probably untenable and certainly likely to result in the same gap between the official and the actual curriculum, between theory and practice, that we have just referred to.

To achieve a common curriculum, or any kind of external control over the curriculum, it is not enough to specify only which subjects it must contain. At present, even in the United Kingdom, as we have already mentioned, this is in practice the situation that holds anyway, since all of the subjects likely to be included in any list that was to have a chance of being agreed are already on the curriculum of all schools. If commonality is really to be achieved, a lot more central direction will be needed than that. It is doubtful if the middle-ground is tenable here.

This brings us naturally to a consideration of the major source of problems presented by demands for a common core to the curriculum — those that derive from what we have said so far about the central role of the teacher in curriculum development and, indeed, the trend towards a recognition of this that we have claimed recent years have seen. We must now turn to a consideration of some of the major facets of this.

The implications of a centralized curriculum for curriculum development

As we have just suggested, a further set of problems appears when we consider what it means for the core of the curriculum to be not only common but also compulsory (Thompson and White 1975). One of the most highly prized features of the English educational system in the eyes of many teachers is the degree of autonomy given to individual schools and teachers. This procedure contrasts most markedly, as we have seen, with the practice of many other countries where a common curriculum is decreed by law.

The objection to this in the United Kingdom comes not only from a desire for the freedom and autonomy that individual schools and teachers enjoy, nor even from an abhorrence of basing educational decisions on economic considerations, but also from the conviction, mentioned already several times, that there can be no satisfactory curriculum development unless this takes place at the coal-face of the individual school and classroom. We have already noted that this would almost certainly result in an individual interpretation of any common centralized curriculum by each school. It also makes the notion of such central dictation not only unacceptable but also perhaps incompatible with the idea of curriculum development in its full sense. Thus many people who accept the full force of the arguments we listed earlier in favour of attempting to offer all pupils a common range of educationally extending experiences would be loathe to accept that this should be done by some kind of central dictation of the content of the curriculum.

We must now look in more detail at some of the facets of this problem. To a large extent we must do this by reiterating many of the points we have made earlier in this book and especially in Chapter 6 about the role of the teacher in curriculum development. For we have assigned him a central role and the proposals for a common curriculum will have the effect of pushing him back towards the periphery.

To begin with, as we suggested earlier, to achieve anything describable as commonality in the curriculum we must reduce the latitude for individual interpretation by the teacher to an absolute minimum. We suggested that it would not make sense to decide on common subjects and leave the choice of methods, approaches, textbooks and so on to the teacher. Thus within the context of any real attempt to establish a common curriculum his role must be reduced to that of a puppet, operated by remote control and able to exercise professional judgement only in the very limited sphere of immediate methodology, if it is possible even there. If we do not accept that this is a proper role for teachers, we cannot accept the idea of a common curriculum, since, as we have tried to show, both logically and practically the two things go together.

One might, of course, react to this point by saying 'So what?'. In other words, it might appear to some that teachers should not be given scope for exercising professional judgement of a wider kind. On the other hand, the central theme of this book has been that the task of the teacher cannot be defined in the kind of mechanistic terms that such a view implies, that education as such can only proceed if teachers are able to make judgements on a much larger scale and that any attempt to inhibit them in exercising this kind of judgement is likely to redound to the disadvantage both of education and of their pupils. One of the strongest arguments for the autonomy of the school and the teacher is that only those on the spot can devise a programme suited to their particular school and its pupils. The experts from outside not only lack this local knowledge, they are also usually people whose expertise is too narrow to enable them to make the kind of holistic judgement that is needed for decisions of practical policy (Dearden 1976). Such holistic judgements only teachers can be expected to make.

Furthermore, we have also argued that it is only through the exercise of this kind of judgement that curriculum development of any meaningful kind can proceed. We examined in Chapter 6 some of the problems of adopting a centre-periphery model for the dissemination of curriculum innovation. We saw the variety of response that there always is from teachers to any curriculum project. We saw the difficulties of getting a project to 'take' in a school and suggested that this could only be achieved if the teachers responsible for implementing it both had a deep understanding of its import and were committed to its ideology, since teachers will only work effectively if they understand what they are about and believe in it. We also suggested that they are most likely to have this kind of understanding and commitment if they have themselves been involved in the planning, the decision-making and the development of the project generally. We even illustrated this point by reference to the disastrous effects that often follow when attempts are made to impose particular innovations or methods, such as mixed-ability groupings, on teachers who are opposed to them.

All of this, if true, implies what we have already said about the variations in interpretation that there will be of any curriculum imposed from outside; it suggests too that such an approach will bring out the saboteurs; it raises the question of whether, as a result, the imposition of a common curriculum is not likely to lead to less efficient rather than more efficient teaching; it also must cause us to reflect that if the central factor in curriculum development is thus rendered largely ineffective, the overall effect will be the ossification of the curriculum.

We are thus faced with a serious dilemma. One solution to this might be to press a distinction we made earlier between central dictation of content and a monitoring of standards. It may be that if we content ourselves with attempting to ensure that certain standards are being attained rather than in specifying in great detail what should be going on in schools, we may be able to exercise the control that some feel to be desirable without unduly inhibiting the teacher in his roles as educator and as curriculum developer. However, we also argued in Chapter 5 that processes of evaluation and assessment themselves have a 'make or break' role in curriculum development. We must now look at this in relation to the idea of a common curriculum.

Evaluation and the centralized curriculum

It has been suggested that there are three types of decision for which the data produced by evaluative procedures is used — course improvement, decisions about individual pupils, and administrative regulation (Cronbach 1963). Where decisions about the curriculum are made by the head teacher and others in the individual school, as at present is the case in the United Kingdom, all three of these aspects of curriculum planning can be and usually are taken together (Stenhouse 1975), and the demands of each, perhaps sometimes conflicting, can be weighed against each other. It must also be noted, however, that where decisions about the curriculum are taken centrally, by school boards, by the state or by central government, as, for example, in the USA and Sweden, the facility to balance these aspects of curriculum development and evaluation against each other seems to disappear and the emphasis tends to swing very much towards the use of evaluative procedures for administrative purposes, to assess the worth of individual teachers, schools or even the school system itself and to measure curricular innovations in terms of what can be recommended to schools as a whole rather than in terms of what seems to be appropriate to the development of the curriculum in any particular school.

Such a change of emphasis must be expected to follow the introduction of any kind of centralized control over the curriculum in the United Kingdom, at least in those areas of the curriculum that become subject to such control. It has several facets.

In the first place, such an approach is clearly likely to lead us back to an objectives model both for the curriculum and for our evaluation procedures. For if we want to know for administrative purposes of the kind we have briefly referred to whether a curriculum works or not, we are inevitably going to begin by stating clearly what that curriculum is supposed to achieve. Thus the pronouncements of politicians on this issue of centralized control over the content of the curriculum and the monitoring of standards of achievement are always couched in terms of their expectations of the output of educational institutions — more scientists, better trained technologists and people who are basically literate and numerate so that they can read the material and do the sums that the jobs they subsequently take up will require of them (but not, one presumes, those that reveal the state of the economy). While admitting the desirability of training a few politicians who were literate and numerate or at least some who could take on the task of getting the state's finances right, we must draw attention to the means/end view of the school's role that is implicit in such statements, some of the dangers of which we examined in our discussion of objectives in Chapter 2 and in our more detailed discussion of evaluation in Chapter 5. It is quite clear that it is this simple model of both the curriculum and of evaluation that we are brought to by the adoption of a system of centralized monitoring of the curriculum.

The second aspect of this is that it raises the whole question of who should undertake the task of evaluation. For the whole thrust of any decision to centralize control of curriculum development is towards an external monitoring of the work and the standards of individual schools or groups of schools. If the results of evaluation are to be used by administrators to help them to organize the work of the schools then clearly they will want to or will be forced to undertake the task of evaluation themselves and to set up their procedures in such a way as to ensure that they obtain the most suitable kind of data from them.

But who is competent to make this kind of judgement from outside the school? We saw in Chapter 6 that the role of the inspector has changed, primarily because of his inability to keep up with the pace of curriculum development in the schools and the difficulties of gaining from the outside the kinds of insight and understanding needed to make a proper evaluation of it. This is still a valid point.

We also suggested that to make it possible for any outsider to do the job we must accept a very simple and unsophisticated view of the curriculum and this is borne out by what is happening as a result of the attempts to establish this kind of accountability in the U.S.A. So many of the dangers which throughout this book we have suggested should be avoided in curriculum planning reappear once external monitoring becomes a central feature of the school system — a clear prespecification not only of behavioural objectives but of those simple objectives that can readily be measured by objective-referenced tests, a reduced 'say' for teachers in the content of the curriculum and in the methods they will adopt, a similarly reduced 'say' for pupils, introducing again the dangers of irrelevance and alienation, the inhibitions on any real educational development that come from having to accept external dictation and external checks on the curriculum, in short, an erosion of the kind of teacher autonomy that we have suggested throughout this book is vital to real curriculum development and educational progress.

The implications for curriculum development of this approach to evaluation were examined at some length in Chapter 5. It should, therefore, be sufficient to note here that this will represent a move away from what we described there as a 'democratic' style of evaluation towards a style that is better described as 'autocratic', or even 'bureaucratic'. We noted before that these distinctions are made by Barry MacDonald from a recognition that evaluation is a political activity. However, the styles described do represent very different ways in which this political activity can be carried out. 'Bureaucratic evaluation is an unconditional service to those government agencies which have major control over the allocation of educational resources. The evaluator accepts the values of those who hold office, and offers information which will help to accomplish their policy objectives' (MacDonald 1975, p. 133). 'Autocratic evaluation is a conditional service to those government agencies which have major control over the allocation of educational resources. It offers external validation of policy in exchange for compliance with its recommendations' (MacDonald 1975, p. 133). It will be plain from these definitions that they approximate more to the style of evaluation that the external monitoring of a common core curriculum will require than does the 'democratic' style.

That style we have noted is defined as 'an information service to the whole community' (MacDonald 1975, p. 134) and its central concerns are to encourage negotiation between all groups who have an interest in a particular aspect of curriculum development and to leave it to the consumers to decide what they will do as a result of the information they have been given; 'the evaluator has no concept of information misuse' (MacDonald 1975, p. 134).

It was within the context of this style of evaluation that we made out a case in Chapter 5 for the teacher as evaluator and suggested that, if the teacher were thus involved both as evaluator himself and as the recipient of information from other evaluators, evaluation could be seen as a central feature of school-based curriculum development, in fact as the kind of action-research that we suggested was implied by that model of curriculum development that sees evaluation as 'formative' or 'illuminative' rather than 'summative'. Such continuous action-research and feedback, allied to the autonomy of schools and teachers to modify their curricula in the light of such information gained or received, was, we claimed, central to any kind of effective and continuous curriculum development.

It will be clear from the preceding discussion that such continuous development will not be possible if the monitoring is done from the outside and if the schools in any case lack the autonomy to change their curricula in the light of what is learnt from it.

The implications of external monitoring, then, for curriculum development are as inhibiting as were those that derived from the external dictation of content. The dilemma remains. Are we to leave everything entirely in the hands of the teachers and risk the occasional disaster when they abuse the freedom this gives them? Or are we to remove this freedom and risk not only inefficiency of teaching and inadequacies of educational provision but also the charge of attempting either to indoctrinate children with a particular system of values or of using them to serve the ends of the state?

One solution to this dilemma that we have not yet explored lies in the notion of accountability. Perhaps we can, as in the Athenian democracy of old, organize things in such a way as to provide autonomy of action but follow it up with some demands that a reckoning be given, that a justification be offered and an account rendered for how that autonomy has been used. We must now, therefore, turn to an examination of that suggestion.

Accountability

There are many people to whom it might be argued that teachers should be accountable, most notable among whom are the pupils and their parents, but hitherto, whenever attempts have been made to render teachers accountable, it is the financial masters, the bodies who hold the purse strings, central or local government that have demanded the right to call for a reckoning.

There are a number of problems associated with the move towards this

kind of accountability, most of which we have already noted in discussing the problems of external evaluation — a return to simple
objectives, a reduced 'say' for both teachers and pupils in determing the
content of their work, a move away from 'democratic' towards
'autocratic' and 'bureaucratic' styles of evaluation and a resultant
slowing down or even arresting of the pace of curriculum development.

All evaluation is political, of course, as is education itself, but this view
of accountability represents a struggle for power rather than for educational improvement or even social advantage, since 'what benefits
members of our society cannot necessarily be equated with what
benefits its most powerful institutions' (Elliott 1976, p. 50).

There are dangers at a number of levels, then, in accepting this
hierarchical model of accountability as accountability to those central
and local government bodies that exercise control over the finances of
education.

Should teachers, then, be accountable to no one? Clearly it is not right
that they should be, although accountability to each other, to their
peers, might be effective enough in most cases. What is needed is for us
to find an alternative model to this hierarchical model of accountability
which will enable us to ensure that teachers accept and fulfil their
responsibilities to society while at the same time not being put under
such constraints in order to do so that they lose the autonomy they need
if they are to carry out their duties as educators in the full sense.

What is fundamentally wrong with the hierarchical model of accountability is that it attempts to make teachers accountable to only one of the
agencies that have an interest in education, or it assumes that
governmental bodies can act on behalf of all interested parties. This is
clearly not so and the only acceptable form of teacher accountability
will be one which makes him clearly accountable to all those people and
bodies that have a stake in what he is doing. This would certainly mean
the involvement of the local community, but it would particularly
imply accountability to parents and pupils.

We discussed briefly in Chapter 6 the role of the parent in curriculum
development and suggested that it might be made greater. We have said
little hitherto about the role of the pupil except in our discussion in
Chapter 3 of the extent to which he might be allowed to choose the
content of his work, but it will be clear that the curriculum is as much
what the pupil makes of it as what the teacher intends (Barnes 1976).
The curriculum only becomes a live entity when the pupil is involved in

it and the curriculum of each individual pupil is the result of what he takes from what is offered (Wilhelms 1962). In the end any pupil's curriculum is an individual one and education is a far more individualized process than we sometimes appear to think (Kelly 1974). Thus, the only real model for the curriculum is one which recognizes the centrality of this interaction of teacher and learner, the model adopted by the Humanities Curriculum Project, the Ford Teaching Project and the Goldsmiths' College Interdisciplinary Enquiry project, all of which were concerned to promote pupil enquiry and thus recognized the important role of the pupil himself in curriculum development. If we accept the importance of the pupil's role, then we must accept his right to participate in the processes of evaluation, as indeed the Ford Teaching Project has done, and thus his right to be regarded along with the parents as one interested party to whom the teacher should regard himself as being accountable.

Teachers are professionally responsible, therefore, to a number of different bodies in society and it is to all of these bodies that they should be accountable. Awareness of this leads to what has been called a 'democratic' model of accountability (Elliott 1976). It has also been argued that the very fact that the teacher is accountable in this way gives him the right to participate himself in the process of evaluation to which his work is thus subject (Elliott 1976). He has a right of reply, even if one is not to put it higher than that, a right that the hierarchical model of external monitoring by government agencies would seem to deny him. Thus we have a model of accountability as a two-way process between the teacher and all of those outside agencies who have a stake in his work. Only thus, it is argued, can we have a genuine system of classroom accountability.

Such a system of accountability acknowledges the central role of the teacher in curriculum development. At the same time, however, it also introduces the idea of the involvement of other interested parties in curriculum development — not only in the evaluation of the curriculum but in the planning that ensues from such evaluation. It requires of teachers that in exercising their central role they take full cognisance of all of those pressures and influences we discussed in Chapter 6 and recognize the rights of other people both to contribute their views on the methods and content of the curriculum and to join in the evaluation processes, provided that this is done in collaboration with and with the full participation of the teachers themselves.

It is in this direction, perhaps, that we must look not only for an adequate scheme of teacher accountability, but also for the only sound basis for true curriculum development. In the last analysis, all education is community education.

Common principles and processes

We have perhaps pointed the way towards the development of a formula which will allow the teacher enough freedom of action to be able to ensure that there is proper curriculum development while at the same time establishing that he is, and must be, accountable to all of those people and bodies who have a stake in his work.

What we have not solved, however, is the dilemma we pointed to earlier when we considered the compelling social arguments both for the establishment of a compulsory common curriculum and for the freedom for teachers to generate different curricula to suit the needs of different children. Do we decide that a part, a core, of every child's curriculum should be common, and thus run the risk of being charged with indoctrination, with imposing the knowledge that we regard as important and, therefore, along with it, its implicit values on all children regardless of their origins, culture, interests and do we try to live with or resolve the alienation that almost certainly will result from this? Or do we settle for working with and from what the child already has and brings to school with him, thus hoping to ensure relevance and meaning to his education but also accepting the generation of different curricula and the possibility that this will result in the continuation not only of the existence of different groups, sections, cultures within our society but also with the social hierarchies that are implicit in them, as some children are given access to high status knowledge and others are denied it?

Two final points are proposed as perhaps offering some clues as to the direction in which a solution to this dilemma may be found.

In the first place, the problem seems to arise from too unsophisticated a view of what the issues are, too naive a polarity. The conflict appears to be between the idea of one curriculum common to all, or at least a common core for the curriculum of all pupils, and the generation of two or three or four curricula, differentiated from each other in terms of broad cultural and social differences between groups of children. Put in these terms the choice is not a difficult one to make, since the idea that there should be different curricula for different classes, races, abilities and so on is quite unacceptable in a society where equality is a stated goal and is clearly repugnant to anyone who accepts the rightness of that goal.

However, it has been argued that equality does not imply sameness and that the confusions we are aware of in the attempts that have been made to achieve equality in education arise mainly from the unsophisticated view that is taken of individual differences between pupils (Downey and Kelly 1975). What we should be contrasting is not the common compulsory curriculum with a system offering two or three curricula, but the idea of one curriculum for all with that of a complete individualization of educational provision. The needs and interests of each child are different, not because he is a member of this, that or the other group, but because he is a unique individual person. To justify making provision for him on these grounds is much easier than justifying providing him with a Black Studies programme because he is black, a secondary modern curriculum because he is 'not an academic child' or a practical curriculum because he is a hewer of wood or a drawer of water.

The practical problems of offering this kind of individualized provision are of course immense both within the classroom and in the wider organization of education, such as, for example, the designing of a suitable system of public examinations, but they are being solved by the current practice of many teachers — the infant schools resolved them a long time ago in far less favourable conditions — and by those who are responsible for the organization of the system. As we saw in Chapter 6, one of the most significant features of the recent development of public examinations has been an increasing move towards individual assignments, special studies, course work assessment and so on.

The practical problems then are there to be solved and are being solved. Theoretically, this kind of approach offers us the only viable alternative to the common compulsory curriculum.

Problems could still arise, however, of a kind that we have seen the proponents of the common curriculum stressing. A narrowing of horizons for the individual or a trapping of him in his own environment and interests are still possible. How are these to be avoided?

Perhaps the answer lies not in attempting to generate a curriculum that is common in its content but rather in attempting to reach agreement on the objectives of all curricula or the principles that will underlie all the educative processes in which we involve pupils.

There can be no agreement over a common curriculum content because of the proper differences that exist between what individuals see as intrinsically valuable and the resultant fact that the road to education must inevitably be different for each individual. If we think of the common curriculum therefore in terms of content, we will always run into major disputes and problems, such as that of defining education in such a way that it will appear to be beyond the reach of some of our pupils. This again was Plato's problem or rather, since we cannot assume he was unhappy with his scheme, this is the problem with his view of education: it is defined in terms of a content so academically demanding as to be beyond the intellectual powers of all but a few gifted people. If we wish to provide education for all, we must recognize that we cannot achieve this by offering all a common educational diet, since this results for some in the kind of disaffection that we have seen described as alienation, in our curriculum becoming meaningless, irrelevant and therefore non-educational or even anti-educational.

If we are concerned that all pupils should be educated, therefore, but wish to avoid those difficulties associated with the theory and the practice of providing all pupils, regardless of their cultural origins, with a curriculum framed in terms of its common content, some kind of solution to our dilemma may lie in an examination of the nature of common curriculum objectives or principles. If we can reach agreement over these — and we suggested in Chapter 2 that at the level of broad principles this may not be too difficult — it should be possible to plan curricula with the reasonable hope of offering truly educational experiences to all pupils.

If there are acceptable broad principles, if education has certain fundamental characteristics that are acknowledged by all or most of those concerned with it, then it is these broad principles that offer the grounds for a commonality of curriculum and it is these features that must be common to the education of every pupil. To deny anyone an upbringing according to these principles is to deny him education, whereas to decide that he need not be exposed to certain kinds of content will not necessarily be to do so. If we can accept that what is crucial is commonality of educational experience at the level of these broad principles, then differences of interpretation deriving from the particular circumstances or views of individual schools, teachers and especially pupils becomes not only acceptable but desirable in respect of and out of respect for the autonomous nature of the educational process. The key consideration is to ensure that these interpretations do accurately reflect the broad principles of recognizing intrinsic value, of developing understanding, of promoting respect for truth and fostering the autonomy of the individual.

This seems to offer a more productive avenue of exploration for those who are concerned at the idea that each child's educational experiences might become too idiosyncratic. There is more likelihood of a consensus of agreement on what in broad terms education is than on what particular bodies of content should be seen as uniquely included in it. There is no one route to education and we must certainly reject the idea either that there are two or three varieties of it or that it is only available to a few gifted people. There are real difficulties, as we have seen, in establishing a common content to the curriculum; these difficulties may not be insuperable if we think in terms of common objectives.

What matters in the last analysis is not whether all children have learnt or experienced subject 'x' or activity 'y', but whether all have learnt to think for themselves, to be critically aware, to see issues in a wide cognitive perspective and, in general, to live autonomous, authentic existences. If that is what is meant by a common compulsory curriculum, then there is no way in which an educational curriculum can be anything else. Disagreement, debate and disaster will ensue, however, if we try to spell this out in terms of a content or a core that is to be common to all pupils.

Summary and conclusions

We have attempted in this concluding chapter to set out the arguments, epistemological, social and political, that have been put and are currently being put in support of the idea of establishing a common core to the curriculum or some system for monitoring the work of schools and teachers. We have also considered some of the difficulties that these raise, particularly those that have implications for the idea of teacher-controlled, school-based curriculum development, the importance of which has been a major theme of this book. We suggested in conclusion that the teacher's central role in curriculum development might be preserved and the need for teacher-accountability acknowledged if a system of 'democratic' evaluation and accountability can be established in which he himself plays his part, along with other interested parties, in the monitoring process. We also suggested that a better route to an adequate education for all might be found if we explore the possibilities of individualizing educational provision while adhering to certain common principles rather than seeking for a common content.

In a sense, therefore, this chapter has been a summary, or perhaps a culmination, of all that has been said in the chapters that preceded it. For all of the facets of curriculum planning which we discussed there — objectives, content, evaluation, the social context of curriculum development — are raised by and have relevance for this issue of the common, compulsory curriculum, so that our final discussion has drawn together a number of threads and thus rounded off our examination of the theory and practice of curriculum development.

Furthermore, in discussing all of these issues, we have been led inexorably to a recognition of the central role of the teacher in all effective decisions as to what in the last analysis the curriculum of any child actually is.

A corollary of this, to which we have also constantly referred and which we must reassert in conclusion, is the need to arm the teacher to meet the demands that this central role makes of him. There are many skills that he needs to develop to respond to these demands. Most importantly, however, he needs a deep understanding of the principles that underlie his work in the classroom. The gap between theory and practice must be closed if teachers are to make full use of the opportunities they are offered. We cannot too strongly reiterate the importance of such an understanding of the theoretical bases of education for every teacher nor, in particular, the value of a real knowledge of curriculum theory.

This must be given a central place in both the initial and the further education of teachers and adequate provision of in-service education must be recognized as crucial to the continuing development of sound educational practice. Teachers cannot be expected to develop their practice to any significant degree unless they have formal opportunities both to acquire new skills and techniques and to maintain continuous contact with theoretical developments.

We have remarked several times that curriculum development requires a deep understanding of the curriculum from within. If the teacher is the only one who is in a position to gain such understanding, it follows that there is a heavy responsibility on him to do all he can to acquire it. It is as a small contribution to that end that this book has been written.

BIBLIOGRAPHY

Archambault, R. D. (editor) (1965) *Philosophical Analysis and Education*. London: Routledge and Kegan Paul.

Ayer, A. J. (1936; 2nd edition 1946) *Language, Truth and Logic*. London: Gollancz.

Bantock, G. H. (1968) *Culture, Industrialisation and Education*. London: Routledge and Kegan Paul.

Bantock, G. H. (1971) Towards a theory of popular education. 251-264 in Hooper (1971).

Barker-Lunn, J. C. (1970) *Streaming in the Primary School*. Slough: National Foundation for Educational Research.

Barnes, D. (1976) *From Communication to Curriculum*. Harmondsworth: Penguin Books.

Bernstein, B. (1967) Open Schools, Open Society?, *New Society*, 14 September.

Bernstein, B. (1971) On the Classification and Framing of Educational Knowledge. 47-69 in Young (1971).

Bloom, B. S. *et al.* (1956) *Taxonomy of Educational Objectives. 1: Cognitive Domain*. London: Longmans.

Blum, A. F. (1971) The Corpus of Knowledge as a Normative Order: Intellectual Critique of the Social Order of Knowledge and Commonsense Features of Bodies of Knowledge. 117-132 in Young (1971).

Blyth, W. A. L. (1974) One Development Project's Awkward Thinking about Objectives. *Journal of Curriculum Studies* 6, 99-111.

Connaughton, I. M. (1969) The Validity of Examinations at 16-Plus. *Educational Research* 11, 163-178.

Cooksey, G. (1972) Stantonbury Campus — Milton Keynes, *Ideas* 23, 28-33.

Cooksey, G. (1976a) The Scope of Education and Its Opportunities in the 80s. 4-13 in Kelly (1976).

Cooksey, G. (1976b) Stantonbury Campus: the idea develops — December 1975, *Ideas* 32, 58-63.

Cronbach, L. (1963) Course improvement through evaluation. *Teachers' College Record* 64, 672-683.

Dearden, R. F. (1968) *The Philosophy of Primary Education*. London: Routledge and Kegan Paul.

Dearden, R. F. (1976) *Problems in Primary Education*. London: Routledge and Kegan Paul.

Dearden, R. F., Hirst, P. H. and Peters, R. S. (1972) *Education and the Development of Reason*. London: Routledge and Kegan Paul.

Dewey, J. (1938) *Experience and Education*. New York: Collier-Macmillan.

Downey, M. E. and Kelly, A. V. (1975) *Theory and Practice of Education: An Introduction*. London: Harper and Row.

Eisner, E. W. (1969) Instructional and expressive educational objectives: their formulation and use in curriculum. 1-8 in Popham *et al.* (1969).

Eliot, T. S. (1948) *Notes Towards a Definition of Culture*. London: Faber and Faber.

Elliott, J. (1976) Preparing Teachers for Classroom Accountability. *Education for Teaching* 100, 49-71.

Elliott, J. and Adelman, C. (1973) Reflecting Where the Action is. *Education for Teaching* 92, 8-20.

Elliott, J. and Adelman, C. (1974) Innovation in Teaching and Action-Research. Norwich: Centre for Applied Research in Education.

Fowler, G. (1977) Uncommonly hard road to the core. *Times Educational Supplement*, February 4.

Freeman, J. (1969) *Team Teaching in Britain*. London: Ward Lock.

Freire, P. (1972) *Pedagogy of the Oppressed*. Harmondsworth: Penguin Books.

Gribble, J. H. (1970) Pandora's Box: The Affective Domain of Educational Objectives. *Journal of Curriculum Studies* 2, 11-24.

Gross, N., Giacquinta, J. B. and Bernstein, M. (1971) *Implementing Organizational Innovations: a Sociological Analysis of Planned Change*. New York: Harper and Row.

Halpin, A. W. (1966) *Theory and Research in Educational Administration*. New York: Macmillan.

Halpin, A. W. (1967) Change and organizational climate. *Journal of Educational Administration* 5.

Hamilton, D. (1976) *Curriculum Evaluation*. London: Open Books.

Hamingson, D. (editor) (1973) *Towards Judgement: the Publications of the Evaluation Unit of the Humanities Curriculum Project 1970-1972*. Norwich: Centre for Applied Research in Education, Occasional Publications No. 1.

Hamlyn, D. W. (1972) Objectivity. 96-109 in Part 2 of Dearden. Hirst and Peters (1972).

Hargreaves, D. H. (1972) *Interpersonal Relations and Education*. London: Routledge and Kegan Paul.

Harlen, W. (1971) Some Practical Points in Favour of Curriculum Evaluation. *Journal of Curriculum Studies* 3, 128-134.

Harlen, W. (1973) Science 5-13 Project. 16-35 in Schools Council (1973).

Harris, C. W. (1963) Some issues in evaluation. *The Speech Teacher* 12, 191-199.

Hicks, G. (1976) Design Studies in Education. Unpublished M.Phil. thesis, University of London.

Hirst, P. H. (1965) Liberal Education and the Nature of Knowledge. 113-138 in Archambault (1965). Also 87-111 in Peters (1973b).

Hirst, P. H. (1969) The Logic of the Curriculum. *Journal of Curriculum Studies* 1, 142-158. Also 232-250 in Hooper (1971).

Hirst, P. H. (1975) The curriculum and its objectives — a defence of piecemeal rational planning. 9-21 in *Studies in Education 2. The Curriculum. The Doris Lee Lectures*. London: University of London Institute of Education.

Hirst, P. H. and Peters, R. S. (1970) *The Logic of Education*. London: Routledge and Kegan Paul.

Hogben, D. (1972) The Behavioural Objectives Approach: Some Problems and Some Dangers. *Journal of Curriculum Studies* 4, 42-50.

Hollins, T. H. B. (editor) (1964) *Aims in Education: The Philosophic Approach*. Manchester: Manchester University Press.

Hooper, R. (editor) (1971) *The Curriculum: Context, Design and Development*. Edinburgh: Oliver and Boyd in association with the Open University Press.

House, E. R. (editor) (1973) *School Evaluation: the Politics and Process*. Berkeley: McCutchan Publishing Corporation.

Hoyle, E. (1969a) How Does the Curriculum Change? 1. A Proposal for Inquiries. *Journal of Curriculum Studies* 1, 132-141. Also 375-385 in Hooper (1971).

Hoyle, E. (1969b) How Does the Curriculum Change? 2. Systems and Strategies. *Journal of Curriculum Studies* 1, 230-239. Also 385-395 in Hooper (1971).

James, C. M. (1968) *Young Lives at Stake*. London: Collins.

Jenkins, D. (1973) Integrated Studies Project. 70-79 in Schools Council (1973).

Jenkins, D. and Shipman, M. D. (1976) *Curriculum: an introduction*. London: Open Books.

Keddie, N. (1971) *Classroom Knowledge*. 133-160 in Young (1971).

Keddie, N. (editor) (1973) *Tinker, Tailor: The Myth of Cultural Deprivation.* Harmondsworth: Penguin Books.

Kelly, A. V.(1973) Professional Tutors. *Education for Teaching* **92**, 2-7.

Kelly, A. V. (1974a) *Teaching Mixed Ability Classes.* London: Harper and Row.

Kelly, A. V. (1974b) The Education of Individuals. *Ideas* **28**, 4-7.

Kelly, A. V. (editor) (1975) *Case Studies in Mixed Ability Teaching.* London: Harper and Row.

Kelly, A. V. (editor) (1976) *The Scope of Education: Opportunities for the Teacher,* Report of a Conference at Goldsmiths' College.

Kelly, P. J. (1973) Nuffield 'A' level biological science project. 91-109 in Schools Council (1973).

Kerr, J. F. (editor) (1968) *Changing the Curriculum.* London: University of London Press.

Kratwohl, D. R. *et al.* (1964) *Taxonomy of Educational Objectives. II Affective Domain.* London: Longmans.

Kratwohl, D. R. (1965) Stating Objectives Appropriately for Program, for Curriculum, and for Instructional Materials Development. *Journal of Teacher Education* **16**, 83-92.

Lawton, D. (1969) The idea of an integrated curriculum. *University of London Instutute of Education Bulletin* **19**, 5-11.

Lawton, D. (1973) *Social Change, Educational Theory and Curriculum Planning.* London: University of London Press.

Lawton, D. (1975) *Class, Culture and the Curriculum.* London: Routledge and Kegan Paul.

Lovell, K. (1967) *Team Teaching.* Leeds: University of Leeds Press.

MacDonald, B. (1971) Briefing decision makers. Internal paper, Evaluation Unit of the Humanities Curriculum Project, later reprinted in Hamingson (1973), House (1973) and Schools Council (1974).

MacDonald, B. (1973) Humanities Curriculum Project. 80-90 in Schools Council (1973).

MacDonald, B. (1975) Evaluation and the control of education. 125-136 in Tawney (1975).

MacDonald, B. and Rudduck, J. (1971) Curriculum research and development projects: Barriers to success. *British Journal of Educational Psychology* **41**, 148-154.

MacDonald, B. and Walker, R. (1976) *Changing the Curriculum.* London: Open Books.

Macintosh, H. C. (1970) A Constructive Role for Examining Boards in Curriculum Development. *Journal of Curriculum Studies* **2**, 32-39.

MacIntyre, A. C. (1964) Against Utilitarianism. 1-23 in Hollins (1964).

Maclure, J. S. (1970) The control of education. *History of Education Society Studies in the Government and Control of Education since 1860.* London: Methuen.

Maslow, A. H. (1954) *Motivation and Personality*. New York: Harper and Row.

Musgrove, F. (1973) Power and the Integrated Curriculum. *Journal of Curriculum Studies* 5, 3-12.

Parlett, M. and Hamilton, D. (1975) Evaluation as Illumination. 84-101 in Tawney (1975).

Peters, R. S. (1965) Education as Initiation. 87-111 in Archambault (1965).

Peters, R. S. (1965) *Ethics and Education*. London: George Allen and Unwin.

Peters, R. S. (1967) In defence of Bingo: a rejoinder. *British Journal of Educational Studies* 15, 188-194.

Peters, R. S. (1973a) Aims of Education: a conceptual inquiry. 11-29 in Peters (1973b).

Peters, R. S. (1973b) *The Philosophy of Education*. Oxford: Oxford University Press.

Phenix, P. H. (1964) *Realms of Meaning*. New York: McGraw-Hill Book Company.

Pirsig, R. (1974) *Zen and the Art of Motorcycle Maintenance*. London: The Bodley Head.

Popham, W. J. (1969) Objectives and Instruction. 32-52 in Popham *et al.* (1969).

Popham, W. J., Eisner, E. W., Sullivan, H. J. and Tyler, L. L. (1969) Instructional Objectives. American Educational Research Association Monograph Series on Curriculum Evaluation No. 3. Chicago: Rand McNally.

Postman, N. (1970) The politics of reading. *Harvard Educational Review* 40, 244-252. Also 86-95 in Keddie (1973).

Pring, R. (1971) Bloom's Taxonomy: a philosophical critique (2). *Cambridge Journal of Education* 2, 83-91

Pring, R. (1973) Objectives and innovation: the irrelevance of theory. *London Educational Review* 2, 46-54.

Rudduck, J. (1976) *Dissemination of Innovation: the Humanities Curriculum Project*. Schools Council Working Paper 56. London: Evans/Methuen Educational for the Schools Council.

Schon, D. A. (1971) *Beyond the Stable State*. London: Temple-Smith.

Schools Council (1967) *Society and the young school leaver*. Working Paper No. 11. London: Her Majesty's Stationery Office.

Schools Council (1969a) *Education through the Use of Materials*. Working Paper 26. London: Evans/Methuen Educational for the Schools Council.

Schools Council (1969b) *Rural studies in secondary schools*. Working Paper 24. London: Evans/Methuen Educational for the Schools Council.

Schools Council (1971a) *A common system of examining at 16+*. Examinations Bulletin 23. London: Evans/Methuen Educational for the Schools Council.

Schools Council (1971b) *Home economics teaching*, Curriculum Bulletin 4. London: Evans/Methuen for the Schools Council.

Schools Council (1971c) *Choosing a curriculum for the young school leaver*. Working Paper 33. London: Evans/Methuen for the Schools Council.

Schools Council (1972a) *With Objectives in mind: Guide to Science 5-13*. London: Macdonald Educational for the Schools Council.

Schools Council (1972b) *Exploration Man: An Introduction to Integrated Studies*. Oxford: Oxford University Press for the Schools Council.

Schools Council (1973) *Evaluation in Curriculum Development: Twelve Case Studies*. Schools Council Research Studies. London: Macmillan Education for the Schools Council.

Schools Council (1974a) *Social education: an experiment in four secondary schools*. Working Paper No. 51. London: Evans/Methuen Educational for the Schools Council.

Schools Council (1974b) *Dissemination and In-Service Training: Report of the Schools Council Working Party on Dissemination (1972-1973)*. Schools Council Pamphlet 14. London: The Schools Council.

Scriven, M. (1967) The methodology of evaluation. 39-89 in Stake (1967).

Shipman, M. D. (1972) Contrasting Views of a Curriculum Project. *Journal of Curriculum Studies* 4, 145-153.

Shipman, M. D. (1973) The Impact of a Curriculum Project. *Journal of Curriculum Studies* 5, 47-57.

Skilbeck, M. (1973) Openness and structure in the curriculum. 116-124 in Taylor and Walton (1973).

Skilbeck, M. (1976) School-based curriculum development. 90-102 in Open University Course 203, Unit 26. Milton Keynes: the Open University Press.

Smith, L. A. and Macintosh, H. G. (1974) *Towards a Freer Curriculum*. London: University of London Press.

Sockett, H. (1976) *Designing the Curriculum*. London: Open Books.

Stake, R. E. (editor) (1967) *Perspectives of Curriculum Evaluation*. American Educational Research Association. Monograph Series on Curriculum Evaluation No. 1. Chicago: Rand McNally.

Stake, R. (1972) Analysis and Portrayal. Paper originally written for AERA Annual Meeting presentation 1972. Republished as Responsive Education in *New! Trends in Education*, Institute of Education, University of Göteborg, No. 35 (1974).

Stenhouse, L. (1969) The humanities curriculum project. *Journal of Curriculum Studies* 1, 26-33. Also 336-344 in Hooper (1971).

Stenhouse, L. (1970) Some limitations of the use of objectives in curriculum research and planning. *Paedagogica Europaea* 6, 73-83.

Stenhouse, L. (1975) *An Introduction to Curriculum Research and Development*. London: Heinemann.

Taba, H. (1962) *Curriculum Development: Theory and Practice*. New York: Harcourt, Brace and World.

Tawney, D. (1973) Evaluation and curriculum development. 4-15 in Schools Council (1973).

Tawney, D. (editor) (1975) *Curriculum Evaluation Today: Trends and Implications*. Schools Council Research Studies. London: Macmillan Education.

Taylor, P. H. (1970) *How Teachers Plan their Courses*. Slough: National Foundation for Educational Research.

Taylor, P. H., Reid, W. A., Holley, B. J. and Exon, G. (1974) *Purpose, Power and Constraint in the Primary School Curriculum*. London: Macmillan.

Taylor, P. H. and Walton, J. (1973) *The Curriculum: Research, innovation and change*. London: Ward Lock Educational.

Thompson, K. and White, J. (1975) *Curriculum Development: A Dialogue*, London: Pitman.

Tyler, R. W. (1949) *Basic Principles of Curriculum and Instruction*. Chicago: University of Chicago Press.

Vernon, P. E. (1964) *The Certificate of Secondary Education: An introduction to objective-type examinations*. Secondary Schools Examinations Council Examinations Bulletin No. 4. London: Her Majesty's Stationery Office.

Warwick, D. (1971) *Team Teaching*. London: University of London Press.

Warwick, D. (editor) (1973) *Integrated Studies in the Secondary School*. London: University of London Press.

Warwick, D. (1975) *Curriculum Structure and Design*. London: University of London Press.

Weiss, R. S. and Rein, M. (1969) The evaluation of broad aim programmes: a cautionary tale and a moral. *Annals of the American Academy of Political and Social Science* **385**, 133-142.

West, E. G. (1965) Liberty and Education: John Stuart Mill's Dilemma. *Philosophy* **XL**, 129-142.

Wheeler, D. K. (1967) *Curriculum Process*. London: University of London Press.

White, A. R. (1964) *Attention*. Oxford: Blackwell.

White, A. R. (1967) *The Philosophy of Mind*. New York: Random House.

White, J. P. (1968) Education in Obedience. *New Society*, 2 May.

White, J. P. (1971) The Concept of Curriculum Evaluation. *Journal of Curriculum Studies* **3**, 101-112.

White, J. P. (1973) *Towards a Compulsory Curriculum*. London: Routledge and Kegan Paul.

Whitehead, A. N. (1932) *The Aims of Education*. London: Williams and Norgate.

Wiley, D. E. (1970) Design and analysis of evaluation studies. 259-269 in Wittrock and Wiley (1970).

Wilhelms, F. T. (1962) The Curriculum and Individual Differences. 62-74 in *Individualizing Instruction, The Sixty-first Yearbook of the National Society for the Study of Education*. Part I. Chicago: University of Chicago Press.

Wilhelms, F. T. (1971) Evaluation as Feedback. 320-335 in Hooper (1971).

Wilson, P. S. (1967) In defence of Bingo: *British Journal of Educational Studies* **15**, 5-27.

Wilson, P. S. (1971) *Interest and Discipline in Education*. London: Routledge and Kegan Paul.

Wittrock, M. C. and Wiley, D. E. (1970) *The Evaluation of Instruction: Issues and Problems.* New York: Holt, Rinehart and Winston.

Yates, A. and Pidgeon, D. A. (1957) *Admission to Grammar Schools.* London: Newnes.

Young, M. F. D. (editor) (1971) *Knowledge and Control.* London: Collier-Macmillan.

Index of Names

Index of Subjects